MW01601597

DEMONISM

VERIFIED AND ANALYZED

First Edition 1922
Hugh White

New Edition 2018
Edited by Tarl Warwick

COPYRIGHT AND DISCLAIMER

FOREWORD

This text is the result of several apparent decades of field work by its author, especially in China, touching on the concept of demonism (to be differentiated, in this text, from possession, strictly speaking, the latter being subjugated to the former.) Noting many dozens of strange cases of sickness, injury, and madness expected to be the result of demonic influence, it is at once a social and religious tract of sorts, in the final chapter encouraging civic action to prevent the problems associated with these spirits.

Dating to a time in which science was still very much underdeveloped and the culture and racial issue very much at the forefront of all academic minds, several claims made here would seem as odd to the religious zealot as to the strictly secular mind of science; namely, that while spirits are both real and potentially dangerous, their action takes place not through some abstract power, but is able to be quantified as a psychological disturbance and can therefore be psychically alleviated by the same, using rudimentary exorcism. Strangely, in proposing this, the text largely refutes the concept of spirits in the ethereal sense, but does touch on the daemon-demon interplay and the importance thereof of differentiating a demon in the Judeochristian sense from, say, a departed ghost.

Some of the content here is based on little more than the then-reigning concept of the less developed regions of the world as blighted for spiritual reasons. It is far easier to care for the soul than to admit that a region is filled with disease and ignorance because of a lack of proper educational institutions, developed medical apparatus, or infrastructure to increase efficiency. When the population actually requires massive expenditures on sanitation and literacy alone it becomes more complex than blaming Satan.

Nonetheless, this particular treatment of the topic of demons is demonstrably more rational than most of its time, even while spurning rationalism as a school itself and questioning the motives of scientists in forsaking spiritual thought. At the same time, the author strikes out several times at spiritualism, apparently supposing that they can lead to possession. He also seems to propose that governments in supposedly demon-blighted nations play a role in encouraging the kind of primitive, "polytheistic" behavior which encourages what he deems psychological disturbances brought on as the eventual effect from the cause of demonic influence.

This edition of "Demonism" has been carefully edited for word usage and has been reformatted as pre-1930s era texts tend to need. Care has been taken to retain all original intent and meaning.

DEMONISM

FOREWORD

Modern Christian civilization has been freed from medievalism- with its demons and witchcraft. An unanticipated byproduct of missionary work is the unique opportunity of applying modern methods to the study of conditions, such as prevailed in past history.

This book was not premeditated. Compelled to come in contact with the demonized, the author found it a necessity to work out the principles underlying the subject. If, thereby, something is done towards unraveling history, towards bringing the spirit world out of the region of the mystic, and into the range of comprehension, of definition, the result will be a distinct advance for scholarship, and Christianity will be stronger than ever. And it is appalling to find that the larger part of the world yet welters in this misery, from which we have been delivered.

The very enlightenment of civilization has hitherto barred the door to recognition, and investigation of the subject of demonism. Out of consideration for readers' difficulties with Chinese names, the cases are referred to by their numbers in the author's records. If called for, these records can be published later.

Hugh W. White

DEMONISM

CHAPTER I

Demonism as a Fact

When the Bible speaks of demon possession, shall we condone it as pardonable ignorance? Shall we berobe, and be-auriole the past as sacred? Is science antagonizing Christianity when it studies demonomania, zoanthropia? I hope to show that, while Scripture and science may view the subject from different angles, they are both concerned with what is a matter of fact.

Incredulity on the subject is not surprising. Men hesitate to believe what they have not seen. In enlightened Christian lands, demonism has been gotten rid of. When missionaries, who find themselves living in the dark ages, claim to have come in contact with demonism, the first impulse is to doubt, not their veracity, but the accuracy of their observations. Snap judgment scouts the subject, or casts the cases into the waste-basket, as a batch of ordinary maladies not scientifically diagnosed. It is true, indeed, that in some cases, a demon has been exorcised with santonin, or pulled out with the forceps- showing merely a mistaken diagnosis. The open-minded reader will, I trust, find herein abundant evidence that demonism is a fact.

I. My records contain three hundred and four cases observed in my own field, sixty-four cases reported by other missionaries, a total of three hundred and sixty eight, besides hundreds of cases incidentally referred to. These are, with a very few exceptions, genuine demonism. A few cases have been collated from Western lands, but they are, as a rule, not demonism.

The cases used to establish the fundamental principles of this book have, most of them, been observed in person by reliable and capable observers. Dr. L. S. Morgan, Dr. James B. Woods, Dr. L. Nelson Bell, Dr. Geo. B. Worth, and Prof. Allison are all accustomed to clinical work, or scientific analysis. Miss Florence M. MacNaughton is an experienced trained nurse. Rev. B. J. Patterson, D.D., Rev. W. F. Junkin, D.D., Rev. Lacy I. Moffett, Rev. James R. Graham, D.D., Rev. Canon Arthur F. Williams, Rev. H. J. Mason, Rev. W. H. Hudson, D.D., Rev. S. Glanville, Rev. Jonathan Goforth, D.D., are trained theologians. One case is by a reliable business man, Mr. John Berkin, C. E. The lady evangelists who have reported cases, having Western education and close contact with the Chinese, know whereof they speak. These ladies are: Miss Margaret King, Miss M. E. Waterman, Miss Florence Nickles, Mrs. Anna Sykes, Mrs. James Bryars, Miss Mary Johnston, Mrs. J. W. Paxton, Mrs. Arthur H. Smith, Miss Clara E. Stegar, Mrs. L. N. Bell, Mrs. J. R. Graham, Miss Mary Culler White, Mrs. H. J. Mason, Miss Janet Hay Houston, Miss Irvine, Miss S. J. Garland, Mrs. W. E. Comerford. Testimony from other reliable witnesses has been culled from their writings.

Such witnesses are: Rev. J. I,. Nevius, D.D., Rev. J. W. Owen, Dr. and Mrs. J. Howard Taylor, Mrs. Johnathan Goforth, Miss A. Mildred Cable, and C. L Butterfield. Of the cases reported in my own field, many have been personally observed and studied. Records have been made immediately, and conditions noted from time to time as the cases progressed. Chinese testimony has been used only as corroborative, or as bearing on details. Such testimony is not used unless sifted and, as a rule, substantiated by a number of trustworthy witnesses.

Some may feel inclined to call for fuller scientific analysis, for clinical examinations, for family histories. Owing to the peculiarities of this malady, such methods are impracticable. I could get plenty of demons for the laboratory, but would put no confidence whatever in a demon which would thus, for pay, allow itself to be analyzed. The testimony brings out a class of cases with well defined symptoms. It is a distinct malady, which I prefer to call Demonism, a term which renders the Greek accurately, and should be objectionable neither to science nor theology. The term Demonsm- or demon possession, if you will- arises from the conviction that when one is so afflicted, a demon takes control of the organs, and the man acts as directed by the demon. It is evident that cases which would not give rise to such a belief cannot properly be classified with demonism. Let us look at a few cases.

My No. 2, I saw in person at the city Funing. She was a quiet, retiring, country woman, of about middle age. When not the demon, she was oppressed, anxious to stay in the mission, and be healed. But, in a flash, the dull features would draw up in abnormal agony, such as no unprejudiced observer could doubt, and in malice, the very demon of a face. The eye would be furtive as of a dog in mischief. She would now be talkative, aggressive, resourceful, malignant. Conversations took place, such as this:

Demon: I did not want to come here. A great many people made me. Have I got to go out empty handed (i.e., without incense or other compensation)?

We: Yes, the Lord tells you to go out.

Demon: (Speaking of the patient as a third person) I am going to take her away. I will not stay here. It does not suit me in this Jesus place. If she stays here, I will not let her eat.

We: Where is your home? Do you live at San Tsao (the woman's home)?

Demon: I live at the Chang Fu Mountain. (There is no

mountain in all the Funing territory.) There are six or seven of us (demons), and all in confinement except myself. If your Jesus can snatch me out, and throw me away, he has power. Have you any way to drive me out?

We: Yes, Jesus can do it.

Demon: Then you will take my life.

The demon was as distinct from the woman as Tom Brown is from Bill Smith. There were alternations back and forth several times a day, at any time, and any where. If there were pathological symptoms, I could not elicit them, i.e., nothing except such as would occur with any one under severe nervous strain. I had several interviews from April 16th to 22nd, 1915. Under our treatment she made marked improvement. Going away for a few days, I came back on the 26th, and was amazed to see her with a smiling face- the first smile I had seen- doing needle-work, and apparently well. But her husband had been anxious when the demon would not let her eat, what scientists call aboulia. When, even after this, she had an attack of it, fearing starvation, he took her away. Authentic report says she finally got well.

The case reported by Dr. Woods, No. 101, occurred in his hospital. The patient was a woman on whom he had operated a few hours before. When he was summoned, she rolled her eyes at him, saying: "I see you, you do not see me. You have not burned incense nor worshiped me." She was not unconscious, had no delirium nor epilepsy. Dr. Woods pressed the superorbital nerve, but saw no proof of hysteria, as ordinarily manifested. She claimed that she was not a woman, refused to be covered up, and demanded incense. He covered her, and replied: "No, we will not burn Incense. We acknowledge Jesus Christ here as Lord, and worship no one else. If there is any spirit in you, he can drive it out." At the name 'Jesus,' she turned on him a curious look, quieted down, the abnormal look in the eye disappeared, and in five minutes she was normal. She was in the hospital ten days longer, and had no further trouble.

One of Miss King's cases, a wheelbarrow man whom she had known for years, No. 108, was diagnosed by a first-class American physician as suffering from tetanus and practically hopeless. When he was sent home to die, the family got a witch. She climbed on the table, went through her incantations, made the patient promise to submit to the demon, and to burn so much incense every year on penalty of further trouble. Shortly afterwards, he pushed Miss King on his wheelbarrow. Now, while Miss King does not claim to be a scientist, she could hardly be mistaken as to what the doctor said, nor as to the fact that a man supposed to be dying of tetanus pushed her on his wheelbarrow.

On May 22, 1920, while preaching, I noticed in the congregation a woman holding a child which looked desperately ill. I always remember it as 'The Skeleton Child.' The poor little thing was nothing but skin and bones. The hands looked like birds' claws. It was crying convulsively. I took for granted that it had some physical disease- demonism did not occur to me. But presently I noticed the fits of crying would come on when we started a hymn. When I examined her, there was no fever, and the pulse was strong. The face showed more malice than agony. When we urged her to say she believed in Jesus, she became angry and tried to strike her mother. The parents said that two days before, when normal, she had expressed faith in Jesus. I recognized it as demonism, and gave instructions accordingly. A few months later, a man walked in with a little child, I was amazed when he said it was the same one. She had recovered immediately after we had seen her.

DEMONISM

Rev, Canon Arthur F. Williams, of New Zealand, having observed the phenomena for twenty odd years, gives data on six cases. One of them, my No. 149, is a most striking case. This was a woman who had been afflicted since childhood, and was supposed to be mentally lacking; At times she was seized by some unaccountable force, and driven into the forest. She was feared as a prophetess and 'ctohunga,' or medium. At forty years of age she was brought to the missionaries, in a pitiable condition, health shattered, ragged and poor. As soon as she was questioned, the face changed and she went off into a trance. The evil spirits were asked: "Who are you?" The reply came in the Maori tongue: "Offspring of the Serpent." The missionaries proceeded to exorcise the spirits, commanding them in the name of Jesus to come out. There proved to be eight or nine, and they came out one by one, giving their names.

With each exorcism the patient would go into a kind of trance, and a voice spoke. The last was an English speaking demon, though the woman herself could not speak English. It resisted, begged to be allowed to go into an afflicted child that was present, threatening to injure the patient's body if compelled to come out. At last it meekly said: "'Yes, I will come out." The woman was thrown bodily off her seat into the middle of the room, where she was suspended in the air at an angle of forty-five degrees, for a period of at least half a minute, and then fell in complete collapse. This occurred in November 19 19. Canon Williams himself saw it, and vouches for the accuracy of the facts. He saw the woman again in 1920, now entirely well in mind and body.

Such cases occur in all parts of China, and some other lands. Many of my cases are from Kiangsu Province. Others are from Chekiang, Hupeh, Honan Kweichow, Rt. Rev. Wm. Banister informs me that while he was officiating in Fuhkien Province many of the churches which sprang up there began with the healing of demon cases. Mrs. J. Howard Taylor and Miss A. Mildred Cablet report cases from Shansi. Nevius reports forty-eight cases from numerous provinces of China and from Mongolia. He and others report it in Japan, Korea, India, Africa, and a case or two in Germany. It occurs in Moslem lands. My No. 152 is a case of epileptoid demonism from Mexico, reported by Miss Houston, a well-known missionary.

In my own field about Yencheng, while we have actually come in contact with only three hundred and four cases, we know the total would run up into thousands. But, to be on the safe side, estimate it at six hundred. As this section has hardly two million people, that would give one to every three thousand, three hundred and thirty-three, or one hundred and twenty thousand for the four hundred million inhabitants of China. It is evident, then, that demonism is a real and well defined condition. It must be classified by itself and studied.

Demonism, as seen today, is the same as in the times of Christ. The terminology is so identical as to make one feel that he is walking the streets of Nazareth or Capernaum. It is a common expression that the demon "vexes" one. The demon talks, comes and goes, throws the patient down, tries to kill him. Let us parallel a case or two. Read the account of the Demoniac ot Gadara. Now consider my Nos. 316 and 118. The former was a widely known demon case. He would have spells. Would go out and sleep in the graves. Would eat filth. Would chant and curse people. He would go to the market, throw off his clothes, and curse with all his might. Now he is well and hearty, thanks to the power of Christ.

No. 118 was a young woman, either demonized or insane, or both. Mrs. J. W. Paxton took Mrs. A. H. Smith to see her. They found her padlocked, and with a heavy chain about her neck, crouching in filth, able neither to rise up, nor to lie down.

DEMONISM

As the patient would break dishes, she was fed from a metal washbowl. She ate like a dog, and licked the bowl. She would call for food all day long, and ate four times during this visit of a few hours. She had spells in which she raved and cursed. In one of them she tore Mrs. Smith's hat to pieces, for which she apologized when the spell was passed. Now she is a quiet Christian, living normally, going to church every Sunday.

In December, 1919, I was at our chapel in the town Tung'kan. The Elder, Li I Cheng, reported that they had lately healed a case like the epileptic demonism of the Bible. It was a woman, No. 387, thirty-five years old. While I was there, she came in and confirmed his statements. She had no occasion whatever to falsify, and indeed the facts were so well known- she lived in a shop on the main street- that there could be no question as to veracity. She told me that she had been troubled ever since the tenth month, sixteenth day, four years before that date. That she would have spells in which she would fall down with convulsions, unconscious. Elder Li said she foamed at the mouth. The spells, as she reported, would last a half hour or several hours.

When not in the actual crisis, she would be unwell and could not eat. In the spring of 1919 she came to the church, her husband supporting her. While there she began to eat. The spells continued but, after she attended church several times, they ceased. I saw her afterwards in 1920, and 1921, entirely well. No. 407 can well be placed alongside the New Testament records. A man was carried to the chapel on a boat in a dying condition. He could not eat, was unconscious, pulse could not be found. There was no sign of life except a faint breathing. After the worship he could walk to the boat with assistance, a week later walked to church, a distance of several miles, and has been well ever since.

DEMONISM

Recognizing, then, that the demonism of today is the same as in the time of Christ, and that both are a matter of fact, we may proceed with analytical study of the subject. Here we find three forks to our road.

I. We may assume that the traditional interpretation of the Bible is necessarily the correct one; that the 'evil spirits' spoken of must be personalities entirely extraneous to the individual, whether the dead or diabolical spirits, taking possession of his faculties, speaking and acting through them in a cuckoo or parasite fashion; that science can throw no light on the subject, and it is merely a question of fact.

II. We may attempt by scientific methods to explain the conditions manifested on a subjective basis as merely pathological or psycho-pathological.

III. We may study the data, study the course of scientific investigations, so far as they bear on the subject, and find out the truth. Are there spiritualities? Can they 'possess' men? And if so, how? As to (I), loyalty to the Scriptures does not necessitate it any more than it would necessitate us to believe that 'de sun do move.' Indeed the Bible in the Greek does not use the word 'possession,' but speaks of the 'demonized,' or those 'having evil spirits.' Past ages, which knew nothing of natural law, attributed everything to direct agency by Spirits. As to 'possession,' the Jews and others believed that the dead could come back to life and 'possess' men ad libitum. Diseases of all kinds were attributed to them, and ghosts walked in all dark corners. The world has outgrown that. We cannot turn back the clock of time.

Furthermore, facts, seen in our cases of demonism, show that this view would lead us into absurdities. In China and Japan many of the spirits claim to be 'The Great Fox Spirit' or 'The Weasel Lady.'

DEMONISM

Rev. Canon Williams of New Zealand states that on one occasion be went into a house to visit a woman. Her little boy was abed with fever. Even before the child saw him, he began to squeal like a pig and kept it up. He would root around under the bedding, and under his father's coat. Williams took the child from the parents, and let him go. He ran about the floor on hands and knees like a pig. The missionary prayed. The child snapped at his hand like a pig, but the squealing had stopped. After a short prayer and exorcism in the name of Jesus, the little fellow jumped up, rushed with open arms, and clung around the missionary's neck. He seemed exhausted, and lay quite still for a while. Then he sat up, and all saw that he was well. Now if the spirits which claim to be a dead relative must necessarily be such, then we must give equal credit to these cases, and animism becomes truth.

Again there are many half-developed cases. We who know them, often recognize a headache or mysterious pains as incipient demonism. Other cases are partially demonism and partially insanity. The first method does not account for these. This line of investigation is unscientific, and would be barren of results. As to the second method, to proceed on the assumption that there are no spirits, and that all can be explained as mere disease, would narrow our viewpoint just as much.

I shall follow the third line of procedure. Science and religion cannot conflict, if they are true. Mistakes of scientists and of theologians slough off as the world grows. Study of demonism proves, independently of religious faith, that there is a Satan, thus confirming the Bible on a point which the world is forgetting. Also we learn the principle on which it would seem that Satan uses evil spirits in demonizing people. These points will be studied further in Chapters VII, VIII, and IX.

CHAPTER II

Demonism vs Insanity

Demonism is just insanity- so says the cursory Bible student. It is the unscientific name for cases of paranoia, epilepsy, manic-depressive, and dementia precox, insanities, such as we see in our asylums- so says the scientist who has not seen demonism at first hand. With such phrases, the world has damned the whole subject as unknown and unknowable. With the facts before us, we should be able, at least, to blast this rock from the path of progress.

Demonism is not insanity in the legal and popular senses of the term. No examiner who knew his business would pass a case of demonism as eligible to a state institution for the insane, any more than he would pass such insanities as delirium tremens or the hysteroneurasthenic quasi-insanities.

Demonism and paranoia are somewhat alike. Even Sidis identifies them. This is more easily understood when we see his view of paranoia as a psycho-pathological decomposition of personality. I hope to show further on, that demonism also is decomposition of personality, but not the paranoiac form of it, for demonism can be healed. When I showed my notes on ten cases to several leading psychiatrists in the United States, they did not suggest paranoia. Nor can demonism be classified with dementia precox. Demonism usually has no 'history behind it,' and shows none of the listlessness, the silliness, the vacuity, the stereotypy, that indicate mental deterioration, Precox is progressive. The healing is never complete nor permanent.

Demonism is clearly differentiated by the fact that it does not usually progress, and can be healed. Nor can the

16

depressives account for demonism, whether as manic-depressive, as what used to be called melancholia, or in other forms. In demonism there is no flight of ideas, no exaltation. Senility does not enter into the case- boys and girls are demonized, The depression of the insanity is inert. There is retardation.

That of demonism is tense. Every nerve is aquiver. In the Shepherd and Enoch Pratt Hospital I was shown a case of hysteria with tense agony like demonism, but the depressives I saw there and at other institutions, all had the hopeless look, the 'lustreless eye' characteristic of manic-depressive. That demonism is not insanity will be seen from some general considerations.

I. Many of the most marked symptoms of insanity are conspicuous by their absence or infrequency. With the demonized the grasp of past and present is good. Memory is continuous, except for amnesia- a break in the continuity of memory- between the periods. Insomnia, distractability, the aphasias have not been observed to any extent in demonism. Of the insanities a large part are to be traced to heredity. Some estimate the proportion as high as ninety per cent. Demonism cannot usually be traced to heredity. There may be several cases in one family, and it passes from one to another of them, but it has a perverse disposition to choose those of no kin, eg. husband and wife, and has an especial affinity for the daughters-in-law.

II. In the well-known forms of insanity, patients usually either die or dement. This term, in the patois of modern institutions, means to become hopelessly demented, regardless of the species of the insanity. It is considered that even in the more hopeful varieties, such as manic-depressive, forty per cent follow one or other of these two courses. Now, among the demonized, death may occur from resultant maladies or from inanition, as there are no stomach tubes among the Chinese. But the proportion of the demonized to die or dement because of the demonism is infinitesimal. I have yet found only two or three cases of the former, and none of the latter. To diagnose as insanity a hundred and twenty thousand or more cases, which do not result in death or in dementing, would be a bold assumption indeed.

III. Demonism usually comes on suddenly, and without previous history, except of environmental conditions. A series of cases to which I shall often refer are my Nos. 323, 324, 325. No. 323 was ill from the first month, lunar calendar, of the year corresponding to our 1918, and died on the eleventh month, eleventh day of that year. Nos. 324 and 325 were her daughters-in law, no blood kin, and were entirely normal. But on the twenty-second day of that eleventh month, they were both taken just as she had been. After terrible afflictions they were healed by Christianity. One of them I have often seen in the two years since, perfectly normal.

The other one also is well. Many of my cases are like these, with no record of abnormalities before or since, yet able to give exact date and circumstances of being taken.

IV. The absolute irregularity and, in some cases, frequency of the periods, differentiate demonism from the insanities most resembling it. It may not recur for two or three years, or it may alternate ten or twenty times a day. The duration may be for several days, or for ten minutes. It may play back and forth like lightning on a summer sky, knowing nothing of periods, or of the rise and fall of the circular insanities. This peculiar form of periodicity is characteristic of demonism. In conversation, Paul V. Anderson remarked that this fact alone would distinguish it from manic-depressive. On February 13, 1921, we began a Bible class at the village Tienhu, to meet every day for a week. On that day, Sunday, after the meeting, a woman, my No. 435, came forward holding a baby. She looked normal and happy. I had not noticed her in the congregation. She said she had been demonized, but was healed, and she wanted us to pray for the baby. While we are praying, all of a sudden the woman herself breaks out shouting as the demon, saying, "Not vex little one, vex big one." The face is now vicious-looking, underlip sucked in, eyes lowering. She turns slowly round and round.

I order the demon to leave her. The reply is, "I have nowhere to go." I order the demon to kneel to Jesus. The reply is, "I will not kneel." But, in a minute or two, I notice a weakening of the patient's aspect, and make her lie down. There is a slight eructation. I tell the people the demon is gone. Presently she goes out with a Christian woman, normal. From Monday till Thursday morning, she is perfectly normal. Talks freely about herself, about this baby, and another child which had died a month before.

The parents believe they were both demonized. We urge her to pray, but she says she is too stupid to learn to pray. On Thursday we attempt to heal the baby. We pray that both child and mother shall be entirely rid of demonism. At this word, the mother is again seized. Some of the Christians take her to another room. When I go there presently, I find her kneeling, the Christians around her, holding a hand and praying. She has thrown off all clothing except the thin undergarment, though it is cold weather. She is trembling violently. When I say that Jesus can drive out the demon, the latter replies: "I am bigger than Jesus- if you do not let me stay here, I will go and stay in some other home." Someone asks, "Who are you?" The reply is, "I rule over heaven and earth." The spell soon passed off. On Friday she came to church normal, but during the service had a severe seizure.

We healed her, and she remained normal until I left there

three days later. Since that she is reported as being well. Now the periodic insanities would not have sudden spells on Sunday, Thursday, and Friday, with the patient absolutely normal between times.

V. A prominent feature, as has been observed by all who have studied the subject, is suggestion. In the cases just given, it is most evident. This shows it cannot be insanity. James K. Hall, of Westbrook, says he never knew a case of insanity, caused by suggestion.

As for the influence of it among the insane, Peterson, Forel, and others tell us the insane are, of all people, the least liable to suggestion, because the attention cannot be fixed.

VI. That demonism must be differentiated from the insanities is evident from the large proportion of the cases which can be healed, and that by purely psychic means. This excludes most of the insanities, especially those in organic terms, brain lesion, focal disturbances, general paresis. Epilepsy and paranoia are generally considered incurable, though epileptoid and paranoiac forms have been cured. Now take my case No. 320, widely known as 'The Wizard.' He and his wife report that his trouble came on originally as an attack of what seemed to be idiocy. He was abed, quite ill for some time, talking idiot-like. Believing it to be a demon, he yielded to the control, and the spell passed off. But he was compelled to practice wizardry, and occasionally would have spells like the first one. This continued for ten years. But he was healed by Christianity. Now his whole appearance has changed, and for four years he has been entirely normal.

My No. 78 is another striking case. A girl of sixteen became afflicted. She was married. The years went by. She became old and wrinkled. Still it continued. Under the influence

DEMONISM

she became a widely-known witch. Her chantings would disturb the neighbors. At sixty-six years a Christian man went to see her. He prayed with her, and persuaded her to take off the nosering, worn as an amulet. She went to church. For several Sundays the demon was especially violent. Then she was healed, and later Rev. C. H. Smith baptized her.

I have often seen her since, well and happy. Note the twinkle in her eye. Now, it a case of paranoia or epilepsy of fifty years standing can be healed by going to church, our institutions would better change their methods.

In distinguishing between demonism and insanity, we must recognize the fact that there may be occasionally a case of insanity wrongly supposed to be demonism. Still more are we likely to meet borderland cases, hard to classify, or showing symptoms akin to both insanity and demonism. Such probably was No. 1. This was a man whom I had known for some time. I baptized him at Funing, on December 9, 1914. When he went home, a relative scoffed at Christianity. He flared up- and was off. I came back on the sixteenth, and the Christians took me to see him. His appearance was that of a man in intense mental agony. He would lie down, sit up, stand- in no position could he get ease. His face was drawn up as in weeping, but I saw no tears. The mouth was frothing and dripping. He recognized me, for once he called my name, like one in agony, appealing for aid. The look in the eye was abnormal.

In the days following, all his thought was about religious matters. He talked about going to hell. Once he heard the incantations of a witch, and was in terror until informed that it was at a neighbor's house. Another time he was scared, because he lost count of when Sunday came. Once he thought he saw a woman, a demon. He followed her, and felt around for her. By praying and the building up of his faith the Christians healed this patient. I saw him often afterwards, well and happy. The only symptom that did not seem to clear up was a tendency to over-emotionalism.

Now this case differs radically from demonism. He had a bright mind, but his constitution had been undermined by opium. In his trouble there was a prominent religious element, but there was no sense of control by a demon. There were no alternating periods. The trouble came at a time of intense mental conflict, the time of change from the old to the new religion. When I reported his case to authorities in America, some considered it hysteria, some manic-depressive; Adolf Meyer considered it schizophrenia, but originating in hysteric conditions. Indeed, the Chinese did not consider it demonism, for they described it, not as demonism, but as a 'disease of the idiocy class.' His affection is hard to define, not demonism, yet not a well-defined case of insanity.

On October 14, 1920, we made a mistaken diagnosis at the 'Kwai' village, a small country place. A child was brought, lying in a flat basket in a wheelbarrow. Several months previously she had come in from the field, suddenly ill. She had then wrapped something around her head, complaining of headache, and crying out in language such as the demonized use. Later, the pains went to other parts of the body; she stopped speaking intelligently, but would occasionally give a sound unformulated. Then she lay down, and since had not been able to rise. In our examination, when the mother threatened to throw her in the river- by no means an idle threat- a flow of tears showed comprehension.

We exorcised and prayed, but the answer came through a dose of santonin. I hear she is well now.

Again, a correct interpretation of demonism, while

DEMONISM

differentiating the species, will recognize it as a psychological abnormality or insanity in the broad sense. A man and a sheep may be classified together if we make the classification broad enough. We may recognize distant relationship with the demonomanias seen in our hospitals. Paranoia, epilepsy, precox, especially of the catatonic class, depressives, especially melancholia- many of the insanities have patients who imagine themselves Jesus, God, the Devil. Religionism is a symptom of many maladies.

The laws of mental science, so far as established, are a help to the understanding of demonism. Nothing is gained, either by denying that it is a demonomania, or by confusing it with the other insanities. Clear analysis is the basis of progress.

As for Bible students, they will be interested to find that when the New Testament sometimes speaks of demonism as lunacy and yet usually characterizes it as a distinct matter, this is not merely a loose of terms. Indeed, it anticipated science. Commentators and translators who have tried to tone down the original Greek to suit their theories have not improved the data.

DEMONISM

CHAPTER III

Demonism Defined

The problem of demonism is now nearer solution than ever before. Science has at last found a key that will unlock it. But to do so, science and religion must co-operate. Neither can alone view the truth from all sides. The key to the problem is found in the principle now recognized by science under various terms, Dissociation, Dual or Multiple Personality, Hysteria.

What is dissociation? Normally constituted, man is an organized whole. Bill Smith or Tom Jones is an intricate piece of machinery, in which physical and psychic factors co-operate, and all according to the principles of natural law. Now the term dissociation is used by some in a wider sense as signifying any nervous or mental irregularity in this organism. In this sense it would include the subject of insanity, already studied. The more specific use of the term signifies the subdividing of the powers and functions of this organism, so that instead of being one organized whole, there appear, as it were, two or more personalities in the same human being, the body being now under the control of one, and now under the control of the other. In these subdivisions the laws that govern the organism still operate to such an extent that each may be able to think and act and speak, appearing to be itself an integrated whole, but neither one has all the faculties and characteristics of the whole, and each has its own distinguishing peculiarities.

Let us take an illustration in the well-known case which Dr. Morton Prince studied under the name Miss Beauchamp. This young lady, of high standing socially and intellectually, was subdivided into three distinct personalities, to which- or shall I say, to whom- were given the names: B I, or 'The Saint,' B IV, or

DEMONISM

'The Realist,' and B III, or 'Sally.' In addition there were B II and other partially formed personalities. The Saint was morbidly conscientious, meek, inconceivably patient, but suffered with neurasthenia, insomnia, depression, fatigue. The Realist, whom Sally dubbed 'The Idiot,' was physically more robust. She was the antithesis of morbid saintliness, as seen in B I, strong, resolute, self assertive, 'sudden and quick in quarrel,' determined to have her own way.

Sally was physically hearty. Let Miss Beauchamp be suffering with abdominal pains, head-ache, exhaustion, and change to Sally. Instantly these symptoms, or rather the consciousness of them, would disappear. Sally could walk miles without feeling fatigue, but afterwards Miss Beachamp would suffer from it. As to disposition, Sally was 'a mischievous, delightful child, loving the out-door breezy life, free from all ideas of responsibility and care, and deprived of the education and acquisitions of the others.' Her anti-conventionality would shock the prudes. Each had memory for the past and clear perception for the present, so far as concerned the one personality. The Saint and The Realist were not conscious of Sally and learned of her only indirectly. Sally was conscious of both of them and spoke of them in the third person. She plagued and teased them, learned even to hypnotize them, and deliberately obstructed the efforts of the experimenter to restore the original. Sally did not know French, but they did.

Alternations occurred many times a day, and often without detectable cause. One of the personalities would find herself, e.g., at the post-office with no knowledge of how she came there. The Saint one day found her mouth unaccountably bitter. She did not know that as Sally she had smoked a cigarette. After years of study Prince was able to get rid of Sally and reintegrate the other two in the original Miss Beauchamp. She is now, as he tells me, a wife and mother, well and happy.

DEMONISM

Dissociation in this sense is generally recognized as hysteria, for science has made wonderful strides in the study of that subject. It is only the Rip Van Winkles who now think of it as necessarily an organic disease, uterine or otherwise. Science recognizes not only that dissociation is hysteria, but that the essential element of hysteria is a dissociating, a limiting of the field of consciousness so that the faculties do not operate as a whole but in a sphere limited to greater or less extent. (Prince.)

This dissociating is psycho-physiological, for the nerve system is the meeting place. It is a functional disorder, a retracting of what are known as the association fibers, so that the more complicated nerve systems of the brain do not function. The psychic limiting of the field of consciousness and the physical retracting of the association fibers are viewed as coordinate. Science now tends to obliterate, or at least ignore the distinction between the psychic and the physical. As for the historic symptoms of hysteria: hyperesthesia, anesthesia, exaggeration, visual irregularities, indefinable coughs and pains, they are now recognized as manifestations of this psycho-neurological condition.

There is a movement to abandon the term hysteria or redefine its meaning. Sidis prefers to use the term 'functional psychosis' as covering this and other conditions. Solomon Meyer, in a paper read before the Chicago Neurological Society, April 26, 1917, urges the abolition of the term. Whatever term or terms come to be used, dissociation belongs in the category of what has heretofore been called hysteria.

My position is that demonism, scientifically considered, is dissociation or hysteria in this sense. To recognize the demon as in reality a subdivision of the original man, as a second personality, at first blush seems antagonistic to the Scriptures. That this is a misconception will appear below, and we make no

DEMONISM

progress so long as the whole subject is involved in a nebulous mist of undefined conditions. In typical demonism there are two well-defined and clearly distinguished personalities, freely and frequently alternating. Each has its own characteristics. Often the voices are distinguishable. In three of my cases, the demon spoke in the northern dialect whereas the normal language of the subjects was Southern Mandarin.

Nevius notes the same. No. 149 is a New Zealand demon which spoke English though the patient herself spoke only Maori.

The dissociating is often marked by abnormal yawning. One of my cases, No. 434, I designate as 'The Yawning Woman.' I first saw her in a meeting being held at Tienhu by Rev. J. C. DeKorne and myself. Knowing nothing about her, I marked her in the congregation as a demon case because she had these abnormal yawns. Being partially healed she was able to keep down most of the manifestations of the demon. This was on December 19, 1920. Since that she reports further terrible struggles, but on February 13, 1921, I noticed the yawns less, and on May 7th they had disappeared and she was well. In narrating changes of personality in the case of Mr. Hanna, Sidis and Goodhart mention the intense sleepiness. ('Multiple Personality' pp. 170 to 187.)

The passing of a spell is often marked by eructations. The Chinese take this to be the departure of the demons. Hence one of their names for demonism, 'breath disease.' On December 31, 1918, at Funing, Elder Iyiu Kwei-rung and myself were called to see a woman. She had been violently affected, drawing a knife on somebody. I found her abed, covered head and ears. When questioned, though a native of the place, she spoke in a Shantung dialect. The face had a drawn expression, rather malicious. She could not eat, would groan, off and on. The

27

DEMONISM

family promised to stop worshiping idols. We sang and prayed. She gave two or three eructations. Soon said she felt first-rate. As we left the house, a witch sitting at the door also took her departure. Sometimes the attacks come on and go off with unconsciousness- syncope- but more often not. There is amnesia, more or less complete, but memory is clear and continuous for each of the personalities. The demon usually knows all about the patient, but the patient may not know about the demon clearly. There is usually no fault in the perceptive powers, and orientation is affected only to the extent of a change of personality.

Automatism is clearly marked. My No. 99 shows, not demonism, but what P. Janet designates as somnambulism. An unusual experience makes a deep impression, an *idee fixe*, and the experience is later automatically reproduced. No. 99, a young man, just baptized, goes with others to a heathen temple. To show his newly-acquired fearlessness, he seizes an idol and attempts to make it stand up. The idol breaks in the middle. The eyes, being loose in the sockets, roll around. The sun, lighting up some red paint, throws a glare over the face as of a flush. A bystander cries out, 'Look, he is crying,' and runs away. No. 99 goes home to tiffin. His meal is disturbed. Going out, he finds in an ancestral shrine nearby a demonized woman. He calls on the name of the Lord Jesus and heals her. But the experiences of the day have been a terrific psychic wrench. He is immediately taken ill.

The broken idol's pains are reproduced in his own waist and he has a headache with tremor, etc. Happily, his faith in Jesus is well-grounded and he soon throws off the bonds of superstition. He has since risen to be a captain in the army.

There are symptoms which some scientists explain as hyperesthesia. In my case No. 29, Mr. Tai was called to visit a woman. Neither she nor her family knew he was coming. Yet when he was three 'li' away, she said: 'That old man is coming,' and talked further about him. Some of the cases chant ditties and refrains not known to them in their normal condition. In one of Miss MacNaughton's India cases, while the demon composed a beautiful poem of several stanzas about the hospital and other matters. Some cases have abnormal strength.

In this form of hysteria the standard tests often do not detect it, for the somatic symptoms are resultant and incidental. Thus in No. 101, Dr. Woods could not detect hysteria from the superorbital nerve. Yet the variety of the somatic symptoms confirms our analysis. I have observed: coughs and hiccoughs; huskiness, dumbness, indigestion, diarrhea, constipation, contractions, paralysis, pains of various kinds, asthma nose-running, frothing at the mouth, blindness, irritation of the eyes, swellings, menstrual trouble, tremor, emaciation, loss of color.

From my records I notice that out of two hundred and ninety-four cases, ninety-nine were men and one hundred and ninety-five were women. As to ages, out of two hundred and ninety-seven, I found seventeen under the age of puberty; fifty which began about the age of puberty, two hundred and eight in middle life, from the twenties up to fifty, and twenty-two old people. As a typical case of demonism, let me relate my No. 58. In a little village lives a Mrs. Ts'wei. She had been troubled with a fox demon for five or six years. She had given up her baby to the care of others. (In my case No. 11 1 and others, the subject under the demon personality has been known to destroy her own children.)

When our people got hold of No. 58, October 26, 1917, she had been abed in an apparently hopeless condition for over a hundred days. Under Christian influence she markedly improved. I saw her first on November 22, 1917. She had then of her own accord walked in to our chapel at the town Tung-k'an, a distance of ten miles. She declared from the first of her intercourse with us a fixed determination to conquer the trouble, saying she would not burn incense to that fox idol if it killed her because she wanted to save her baby from such a fate. I found her to be a woman of about thirty years of age. From the 22nd to the 25th in the preaching services and otherwise we observed her carefully. The spells would come on frequently, more especially during the singing and prayers. She would be sitting quietly. The face would begin to look surly and the lips to pout. The left-hand corner of the mouth would draw down. As she got more deeply under the influence, malignity and hatred would show in the countenance. The head would weave, if we may borrow language from the elephant. Sometimes there was weeping. She would begin to yawn and continue it a number of times, each orgasm more tense than the previous one, until with the final expiration she would give a scream, possibly the automatic reproduction of the fox bark. Once I heard it on an intake of breath. It is the only case in which I have heard this scream. The spell now on, she would chant in the voice and personality of the demon, saying, e.g., "There were a hundred and twenty-five of us (demons) when we came, but now there are only five. For three years we have eaten good food, but they will not burn incense to us any more. How many people have they anyway? (Seeing the crowds of Christians coming in from the country.) I must take her away from this place. But where shall I take her? She has kinfolks at Funing, T'ien Tsi-ts'ang, and Tung-k'an, but they have chapels at all those places. Alas, for my life! Alas, for my life!"

On the morning of the 24th, the demon was saying: "Go on home. I will spare your physical life." The subject in her own personality would reply; "No, I am not going home." The spells would pass off quietly. Between times I would see her doing needle-work or helping about the kitchen. When I would talk to her casually, she would reply normally, but sometimes seemed to shun me.

We tried to get her to pray to Jesus. She replied to me: "He (she or it) will not let me say it." She would start to repeat a prayer, but when she got to the name "Jesus," she would balk. I learned later that on the 27th, after I had gotten away, under the repeated efforts of the Christians she did get it out, and then kept on repeating it. Before I left, on the 25th, while Mr. Tai was preaching, the demon was much in evidence, the face twisting and twitching, with continued chanting, and now and then yawns and screams. When I rose to conduct the baptisms and sacrament, she was quiet and looked normal. When we came to the final hymn and prayer, I anticipated trouble, but to my astonishment, there was not a sound, and the face had an entirely new aspect. She looked completely subdued. Instead of the hard lines and contractions of the lips, the face looked relaxed. The mouth would open and shut by the dropping of the chin as of one in extreme gasping for breath.

During these interviews, the minds of the Chinese were confused by the question whether this trouble was due to phlegm- they have an idea that mental aberrations come from this source. Our ancestors had theories no less ridiculous. On December 22nd, the husband brought her to Yencheng for diagnosis. They came to the morning service, much to the amazement of the congregation, most of whom had never seen anything like it. While I preached, the demon was in evidence as usual. The medical man, J. W. Hewett, sat down by her and by speaking softly tried to quiet her. Being now the demon, she turned on him viciously like a snapping dog. At one time, when she became especially vociferous, I went down from the pulpit, laid my hand on her shoulder, and in an authoritative voice, said: "Jesus Christ commands you to come out of her. Are you not going to do so?" The demon immediately quieted down, whimpering: "Alas, my life is done for. They will not burn incense to me. That man 'Kwai,' that man 'Kwai,' and this Mr. White! I am afraid of them." 'Kwai' was the neighbor who had first brought Christianity to bear on her. On Monday the 23rd, the husband and wife came to my study. They talked for fifteen minutes. She was perfectly normal and had no trouble while there. On March 16th and 17th, 1918, at her own village she told me that she had no further trouble in her everyday home life, spells coming on only in church. I noticed twice on this occasion that when a spell came on, she could control it by her own volition. She now talked normally and smiled, the latter an especially good indication of progress.

To obtain the judgment of the best science, I sent my notes on ten cases to a number of experts in the United States. Lewellys F. Barker wrote: "This is a valuable series of cases and they fall into groups with which we are now- thanks to modern psychiatric study- fairly familiar. Most of them are cases of dissociated personality, that come in the definite hysteria group. A few of them are probably instances of the manic depressive psychosis. It is possible that some of them belong to dementia precox, but this is less likely."

Morton Prince wrote: "They are plainly cases of hysteria. In principle they are well-known. More specifically, the phenomena are manifestations of subconscious ideas, known as sub-conscious personalities."

We must, however, differentiate demonism as a type of dissociation *sui generis*.

I. Dissociation as distinct from demonism is rare. P. Janet tells his Harvard audience the subject is so rare that they will hardly have to deal with it in their practice. Dana in 1894 found in all literature sixteen cases. Prince in 1906 charted twenty cases. Others have been discovered since, but in no considerable numbers. In 1917 I visited three well-known institutions for nervous and mental cases, one of them, the Maryland Hospital for Insane, having over eight hundred cases. In neither of them did I find at that time a case 'of dissociation, though in the latter the superintendent, Dr. J. Percy Wade, had observed it previously.

Now demonism occurs only under certain conditions, but given these conditions it is widely prevalent. To diagnose it as dissociation or hysteria of the general type does not account for the one hundred and twenty thousand or more cases in China alone. It is essential to qualify our diagnosis. The clear demarcation of localities gives us one differential, that it is of environmental origin.

II. Certain uniform predominant traits differentiate demonism. In the insanities which occasionally show dissociation, the variety of the concepts personified is unlimited. They cover the whole range of the human mind from a rooster to Almighty God. Variety is also to be observed in the cases of hysteric dissociation. Miss Beauchamp had her 'Saint,' 'Realist,' and 'Sally.' Mollie Fancher, studied by AH. Dailey, had her 'Sunbeam,' 'Idol,' 'Rosebud,' 'Pearl,' and 'Ruby.' Doris Fischer, studied by Walter F. Prince and J. H. Hyslop, had her 'Margaret,' mischievous, 'Sleeping Margaret,' benevolent, 'Sick Doris' and 'Real Doris.' Alma Z., studied by Osgood Mason, had her 'No. I,' intelligent, patient, womanly, but with illness and pain. She had her 'Twoey,' a bright, sprightly child, ungrammatical, Indian as to character, shrewd, interested in the well-being of 'No. i.' Then she had a third personality, 'The Boy,' broad and serious, lacking in all the book knowledge of 'No.1' but interested in politics and practical matters, and a good housekeeper. In some of the cases studied there have been two clearly defined personalities but no one trait so predominant as to name them. Such are the Mary Reynolds case (Weir Mitchell), Marcelline (J. and P. Janet), Felida X (Azam).

Variable symptoms do not differentiate species, but uniform traits, appearing in a definite, well-defined class of cases would. The bumble-bee of China has a different stripe from the American varieties; the pigeon has a different note, the bull-frog has a different croak. Yet the bee is still a bumble-bee, the pigeon is still a pigeon, the frog is still a frog, for there are uniform traits which differentiate the species, regardless of minor differences.

Now demonism may vary in details, but it is differentiated from other forms of dissociation of personality by the uniformity of certain traits, eg, there is always a sense of control and the control is always conceived of as a demon. In some of my cases, the demon represents the superstitious concept of the Fox or Weasel spirits. In No. 3, a young married woman was afflicted with what appeared to be the spirit of her father-in-law. No. 26 was supposed to be an enemy seeking vengeance. Various gods and spirits are represented, but there is always the demon idea- using demon in its original non-moral sense. Other uniform traits are; demand for worship, antagonism to the name Jesus, etc.

III. Demonism is differentiated by the morally evil quality. Let us be clear. In other forms of dissociation, abnormal evil, malice, ferocity appear. But in many cases it does not. Take that case of Ansel Bourne, studied by Professor James. An itinerant preacher, sixty years old, in his usual health, living at the town of Greene, Rhode Island, he suddenly disappeared. Two months later he was found at Morristown, Penn., keeping a store in the name of A. J. Brown. He had appeared to the neighborhood as normal. When became to himself, he did not remember the Brown episode until James brought it back by hypnotism. Here there was no moral element. (N.B. I use the term moral only in its ethical sense. Dubois, P. Janet, and others use it in what the Standard Dictionary calls a looser sense, embracing intellectual and emotional elements.) Both as Bourne and as Brown this case was religious, morally good. Would anyone claim that Sally was morally evil?

Prince expressly disclaims it, and says that dissociation does not usually cleave along moral lines. Compare the 'B' personality of 'B.C.A.' and 'Twoey.' In some cases, as Marcelline and Blanche W., both studied by Jules and Pierre Janet, not only is there no moral quality but the second is superior to the first as to both health and temperament. Blanche W. in the second personality passed examination as nurse though she could not do so before. Indeed, in some of these cases the operators have left patients in the second personality, recognizing that as normal.

It is evident that in dissociation per se the dis-aggregated self may be morally good, morally evil, or morally neutral, as the case may be. But demonism would not be demonism if the morally evil trait were left out. It is this trait which has in all ages led men to attribute it to Satanic agency. In the data now available, the evil trait is either universal or so general as to be distinctive. Partially developed cases, of course, do not show all the symptoms, but every fully developed case I have observed manifested the morally evil quality. Should a sporadic case occur without it, our proposition would not be disproved. Diphtheria sometimes kills, even though the diagnosis does not reveal it.

The evil quality may manifest itself in various ways. Thus Miss Waterman, in giving a ferry-woman's case, No. 105, says: "When the spells come on her, there is a distinct change in her disposition and appearance. At other times she may be normal and pleasant. But at times she gets a dare-devil, defiant air, talks in a different voice, she lives a profligate life, and says she cannot help it, that the influence compels her to. Sometimes she goes away from home for several days, and when she returns, says the demon was working in her so that she could not but go."

Another form of moral perversity shows out in a series of cases reported from Sutsien, Kiangsu, by Rev. B. C. Patterson, D.D. With these cases, wherever they go, fire breaks out, a phenomenon observed sometimes in the insanities. One of these, the Tusan Girl, No. 120, had not been in the mission chapel twenty-four hours before a neighbor's house caught fire. Dr. Patterson and his colleagues did not dare bring her into the central station, but the Roman Catholics took her in, guarding against danger by putting up an image of the Virgin Mary. In a nearby room a teacher's clothes caught fire, and presently the mat on which the girl slept was afire.

The actual causation of these fires we must attribute to the abnormal ingenuity of the demonized and we are not surprised that the Catholics found a box of matches on her. But the psychic symptoms accord with what we know of demonism. The more common form for the evil quality to take is that of malice. My No. 323 died of the demonism, as mentioned in Chapter II. Five days later a daughter in law of that family, No. 325, woke up to find her two months old baby dead on the bed. Four days later this No. 325 and another daughter in law, No. 324, became afflicted with symptoms similar to those of the mother in law. The demon represented itself to be the 'Weasel Lady,' the spirit which "contracts the sinews and skins the hide," IE, in vengeance for the sufferings of the weasels. It said: "I have strangled two of them, a big one and a little one, and I have three more to get before I am through." When I saw No. 325, her face between spells looked wan and distraught. When the spells came on, she would begin to yawn and then the face would be drawn up in anguish. The family were in misery, pursued by this nemesis until relieved by Christianity. This malice pervades most, if not all of the cases.

A distinct stigma necessitates a sub-classification, in the genus Dissociation of Personality. Let us take a supposititious case. In Central Asia arises a malady. It is characterized by symptoms physical and symptoms psychic, sometimes repeated but not uniform. It is noticed, however, that of those reported practically all manifest an abnormal bravery. This characteristic appears in old and young, in male and female. The malady spreads. It appears in many lands and always exhibits this trait. Science would not hesitate to recognize this as a distinct malady, differentiated by the quality bravery. So to differentiate demonism by the morally evil quality is not religion but science.

In the normal personality there are rudiments of a cleavage along moral lines. Sidis has brought out the fact that the normally constituted mind has certain inhibitory, or as he calls them, guardian faculties. When stimuli are presented to the mind, these faculties must determine whether or not the psycho-neurological system shall respond to them. These inhibitory faculties, insofar as they have to do with moral qualities, correspond to what theologians call the 'moral nature.' They define this moral nature as a quality of the mind. These inhibitory faculties are constantly coming into contact with stimuli of a morally evil quality and conflict arises.

The consciousness conceives the combatants as two men, the 'old man' and the 'new man,' the 'flesh' and the 'spirit.' These two men are what Prince would call 'systematized complexes,' and dissociation usually follows the lines already thus systematized in the normal personality. In demonism this evil nature gets control of the man. In his normal condition it works against his better nature, obstructs his highest development, but it is held down by the reason, the conscience.

DEMONISM

In this form of dissociation, the servant gets control of the master; Mr. Hyde, the Mr. Hyde that lies unknown in every man, takes control of Dr. Jekyll's body and becomes the demon. In other forms of dissociation the moral faculties may be affected incidentally, but the fundamental cleavage is not along moral lines. Sally would be a very mild demon indeed and Twoey a benevolent one.

The question may be asked, Is not demonism the same thing as the trances of the mediums? Yes and No. Motor cars are all motor cars but some are Fords and some are Buicks and some are Hudsons. The banker uses one for his private business, the jitney runs for the public, and the trucks carry milk and coal. The principles of dissociation run through multiple personality, spiritualism and demonism. Yet the distinctions given above clearly differentiate demonism from all other forms of dissociation. It is for us, as we go forward, to find out whether demonism is a Ford or a Buick or a Hudson, and what part it plays in human life.

Having thus analyzed demonism as dissociation, morally evil, let us not jump to the conclusion that we have accounted for it on a subjective basis. The crux of the problem is yet before us. Whence come these evil traits? Whence come the abnormal faculties of the demonized? Can the thought-content of these dissociated personalities, and the abnormal psychic attitudes be accounted for on a purely subjective basis? How comes it that the morally evil nature, ordinarily under control, now throws off the inhibitory faculties, the conscience, the will, and the servant becomes the master? Is there outside influence, and if so, by whom?

CHAPTER IV

Demonism of Psychic Origin

When we analyze demonism as hysteria traditionalists may take a shudder as though we had cut under the Bible. Independent thinkers will grasp the idea. Granting it to be, in a sense, a disease, the origin is not to be traced to some germ or blood clot or lesion. This chapter is written to prove that demonism comes preeminently from psychic causes, IE, from the mind. The question, What affects the mind, will be taken up later. There are, of course, often physical conditions which make one more liable to demonism. Dr. L,. S. Morgan reports that the cases which come to his hospital usually show some physical ailment.

One of his cases, No. 102, was unable even to sit up without assistance. She could not eat and was amazingly wasted. Aside from the 'demon,' which was, to her mind, very definite, moving about from place to place, he found indefinite symptoms such as would occur with functional indigestion. Another of his cases, No. 103, had a bad mitral insufficiency. He treats his cases with drugs, as the symptoms may indicate, but says he depends more on influencing them through the Bible women to get rid of the demon idea, to use the treatment, and above all, to believe in Jesus. No. 102, as he reports, laid hold on the power of God by prayer and was healed. She used the medicines for a while, and then dropped them. Later she was baptized and now for several years has been an active Christian. In healing No. 103, digitalis played a prominent part, and when threatened with recurrences it still helped her. After recovery she had a fine baby.

The dissociations seen in Western clinics usually occur with disease, though even this may be psychopathic. Barker says of hysteria: "Most patients have a distinct neuropathic or psychopathic predisposition." Prince found in Miss Beauchamp's case an inherited nervous instability which prepared the way for the dissociating when she received a severe nervous shock.

Happily science now knows what hysteria is, a functional condition of the nervous system and this nervous system, the meeting place between mind and matter, may be affected by either physical or psychic causes. For the causation of psychopathic conditions generally, Adolf Meyer gives a five-fold classification. He says the disorders may be: I; Exogenic, caused by, e.g., alcoholism or sexuality. II; Organogenic, arising from some disease of an organ other than the brain or nervous system, e.g., thyroidism. III; Neurogenic. Such conditions are seen where we can actually demonstrate some nervous disorder such as a brain lesion. IV; Psychogenic, arising from life experiences, shocks, etc. V; Constitutional, the most lasting characteristics, whether derived from heredity or acquired.

From this we see that his position, which we may say represents the general scientific opinion, is that with some nervous or mental diseases, a break-down, an insanity, may with one patient be caused by, EG, drink, opium, or disease of the thyroid glands, whereas with another patient the identical disease may come from the shock of a mother's death or from an attitude of the patient's mind due to unfortunate relationships in the family.

For hysteria the trend of opinion is to stress the psychic rather than the physical causes. In his chart Meyer questions whether it is to be found under the first three headings, but does find it under the last two, in which the psychic element is prominent. Indeed, in cases where the physical factor would seem most clearly indicated, as where dissociation occurs after a railroad accident, Prince attributes it rather to the psychic than the physical shock. In the well-known case of Mr. Hanna, the dissociation came from a fall, which we of the laity would consider a physical cause.

Yet the scientists healed it largely by psychic means. Physical conditions, where they occur, are now considered excitatory rather than efficient. This is true even of the sex organs which formerly bore all the blame for hysteria. So, EG, say Dubois J and Stoddart.and Sidis in his latest work, 'The Causation and Treatment of Psychopathic Diseases' says: "In all functional psychosis" (in which he includes hysteria)... "there must be a mental background, and it is the mental background alone that produces the psychosis and determines the character of the psychopathic state." (italics his.)

We may, then, infer that with demonism, while physical factors may be present, the psychic must be the predominating etiological factor.

We may go yet further and say that demonism may be caused entirely by psychic causes. In conversation Prince called my attention to the fact that the mediums, whose stances are dissociation, are trained to this work. This form of hysteria is by some classified as artificial, thus distinguishing it from the hysteria occurring with diseased conditions. It is hypnotism. The Nancy School of psychiatrists proved to the satisfaction of the world that persons could be hypnotized who had no hysteria, congenital or otherwise. Indeed Babinski would not recognize as hysteria anything which could not be produced by suggestion.

That psychic causes are entirely adequate to produce dissociation is evident from modern researches. Dubois gives an interesting incident. A professor was demonstrating before his class. By chance a patient came in with a trifling ailment. Treatment was given him. The professor then asked, "How long is it since your arm was paralyzed?" The patient, who was perfectly well, denied any such thing. The professor insisting, paralysis actually took place and continued until relieved by counter-suggestion.

P. Janet reports a man blind for four years, a woman blind for two years, and another with frequent attacks of blindness for a few days at a time, and all of psychic origin. A popular magazine reports a case of blindness diagnosed and relieved on psychic principles by Dr. Ames of New York. Among Charcot's cases, one, a man of forty, found that his wife had disappeared, taking their funds with her. He lost speech for eighteen months. Sidis brings out the psychic origin of asthma. Also with a patient, who for years had had his stomach washed and dosed by physicians, who had suffered with fainting attacks, indigestion and serious heart trouble, the disease was diagnosed by Sidis as originating in fear. Epileptiform cases, neuralgias, etc., have been traced to psychic shock. With such evidence before us, we have scientific basis for our position that demonism may be caused by the mind, whether the patient has or has not any physical disease.

Now let us take up our data. We see China full of demonism, while Europe and America hardly know there is such a thing. There must be a cause, a cause uniform and adequate to account for conditions. To illustrate, Newtown and Middletown are twelve miles apart. Soil, climate, race are the same. In Newtown occurs a case of typhoid. In Middletown none occurs, or a sporadic case. The man who would trace one case to a cold, one to a fall, and one to upturned earth would soon find himself classified with a rather malodorous species of the genus homo. A cold or a fall might predispose to typhoid but for the cause we must search the water, the food, the local conditions which have influenced all the cases. Let us see whether a physical cause can be found which would affect all these cases of demonism.

DEMONISM

The pre-dominance of female cases at once suggests the old idea of a uterine disorder as the cause. In a number of my cases, the demon was more marked with the menstrual periods. At Tung-k'an, November 1917, a young man, No. 71, came before the session. He was a partially healed demon case, though the wan face, disheveled hair, and generally lackadaisical appearance emphasized the 'partially.' His wife No. 72 was reported as a more serious case. She would be normal and all of a sudden would break out cursing and mocking at people. Once as the demon, she struck her neighbor, who was also a demon, No. 58, saying, "You are no good any longer. They will not burn incense to you now."

As the demon she spoke Northern Mandarin, whereas her normal dialect was Southern Mandarin. In March 1913, when the husband came into the room, he was so hearty, tanned, jovial, that I could hardly believe he was the same person. But the wife, a nice looking young lady of twenty-four, could claim to be healed only two weeks and there was still question about her. They reported that her menses were delayed and they had no child, though they had been married three years. It would look as if the intensity and the prolongation in her cases were due to physical causes. But on the other hand, with my No. 5, the healing of the demon by prayer and faith was immediately followed by conception. Her little boy, born soon afterwards, was witness to the fact that with her the physical symptoms were resultant rather than causal.

With No. 3, a young wife had a demon which came on with the menses. A tremor would go over her. She would groan twice. Then the demon would be in control, talking and chanting. Any physician of the old-time regime would have diagnosed it as veritably hysteria- a disease of the uterus. But when she was healed the trouble immediately took her husband, a hearty young farmer, and now for four or five years he has been afflicted with it.

No. 364 was another noteworthy case of demonism in a male. On November 6, 1919, in our chapel at Tat'ao, I noticed a man, who had been brought on a barrow. He looked very ill. When they supported him into the room, he sat motionless for two hours. In the examination he reported that he had been ill for two months. He had not eaten, to speak of, for ten days. Did not urinate. Presently he began to breathe very hard. I told him to lie down. He did so, beginning to moan. After the meeting they took him away on a barrow. I saw him in December, 1920, robust, ruddy, strong.

Demonism is just as serious with males as with females, but it occurs more often with the latter. This must be attributed, not to the physical, but to the psychic feminine. True, the psychic feminine is influenced by physical conditions of her sex. Note the irritability of the pregnant woman. Indeed, we may say that fear of a mouse may be attributed to woman's sex, as so many women do fear a mouse. But a man may be irritable and may even fear a mouse. If we fall in line with the trend of opinion, and consider demonism as a psycho-physical condition of psychic origin, the pre-dominance of it among women is easily accounted for on the principle that the psychic characteristics of woman are such as to render her peculiarly liable to demonism. This hypothesis gives no embarrassment when a case occurs among males.

In writing the above, as the most typical case of demonism arising probably from physical sex conditions, I selected No. 72. On May 22, 1920, some time after this was written, I went to her village, and what was my surprise to find No. 72 rejoicing in a baby! The healing of the demonism had healed also the sex trouble, thus showing that the latter was not the cause of the demonism but the result of it.

DEMONISM

Can heredity account for demonism? Possibly in some cases it may predispose to it. Meyer recognizes it among the constitutional factors possible in hysteria. But Sidis denies that psychopathic diseases are hereditary. In my cases, heredity has not been noticeably prevalent. Even where it seemed most clearly indicated, there were usually decisive reasons for not recognizing it as the efficient cause. Where several cases occur in one family, it usually passes between those of no blood kin, as the husband and wife, and it especially prefers the poor daughters-in-law.

My No. 67, while a maiden, worshiped a large paper idol, and became afflicted with demonism. After marriage it persisted. Whenever she omitted the burning of incense, she would feel badly, would then not recognize her husband and would talk as the demon. After she had been oppressed for twenty years, a neighbor became a Christian and took the preacher to see her. He found this idol treasured up in the bedroom, showing thereby unusual devotion, for the idols usually hang in the sitting room. She allowed him to take it down and was soon healed. But she had a son eleven years old. After the healing, one day an idol procession was passing. He joined in and from that date the demon came on him. After a year or more, he too was healed. Then his sister-in-law was afflicted. In these cases the three all manifested the same symptoms, including, what is not so common, vomiting and purging. Now, was the son's case due to heredity?

If so, how explain the evident connection with idolatry? How explain the daughter-in-law's case? How explain the fact that neither of these cases occurred until the mother was healed?

On the question of etiology, epilepsy needs especial elucidation. The appearance of epilepsy among the demonized and possibly of demonism among the epileptic, has in this hitherto unanalyzed subject led to hopeless confusion. What is epilepsy? Science is not prepared to commit itself. But the trend of opinion is to put epilepsy among the diseases expressed in organic terms. Spratling interprets it as organic and Dunton, of the Shepherd and Enoch Pratt Hospital, accepts his opinion on the ground that the marked increase of neuroglia fibers necessarily implies degeneration in the tissue of the brain. The general opinion that epilepsy is incurable rests, of course, on the interpretation of it as organic.

There are, however, diseases recognized as epileptiform, to say the least, which are of psychic origin. Sidis gives an interesting case. A Russian, twenty-one years of age, was affected with what appeared to be Jacksonian epilepsy. There would be rhythmic movements, convulsions, anesthesia. The head and the whole right side were affected. The attacks would come on annually, about the same time, and would always begin at midnight. On being examined under hypnosis, the trouble was traced to an experience in his sixteenth year. He was then in Russia and very superstitious. Going to a ball one night, as he passed the cemetery, he thought he heard somebody after him. In fright he fell down and had a 'fit,' being carried home unconscious.

Under hypnosis he would live this experience over. Again he was in Russia, talking Russian, talking about his mama, frightened to death and having a fall. The psychopathic origin of this epilepsy was clearly demonstrated. Such epileptiform phenomena are especially frequent with hysteria.

Now true epilepsy may manifest dissociation. In Prince's chart, a number of the cases of dissociation were epileptics. But to my inquiry about them. Prince replied that the dissociation was one thing and the epilepsy was another. Demonism, being a species of dissociation, may be induced by epilepsy- though I have not yet found any such cases. On the other hand, as demonism is hysteria, it may manifest itself in epileptiform attacks. Such cases are beautifully paralleled by Sidis's Russian. Among my cases, a number manifested the demonism in this epileptiform way. No. 134, reported by Mrs. J. R. Graham, when in the spells turned a distinct purple color. No. 387 for over three years had been liable to spells in which she would fall down unconscious, having convulsions and foaming at the mouth. No. 440 was a young man. When the Christians were summoned, they found him abed, unconscious, mouth contracted and foaming. Yet we heal these cases by faith. No. 387 got well by coming to church and has continued well for two years. No. 440, three months after our healing, is working in the fields and preparing to get married.

See Breuerfand Freud's 'Studien uber Hysteric.', "Journal of Abnormal Psychology," October, 1906.

Whether the demonism be super-induced on the epilepsy or the epilepsy be a by-product of the demonism, in any case epilepsy cannot account for demonism as the great majority of the cases are curable.

Of the numerous maladies seen with demonism, the eye cases attract attention. For the benefit of scientists I will give a few cases rather fully. No. 348 is a little boy. According to the statements of the father, mother and others on the fourth day of the second month, lunar calendar, 1919, in the morning the boy was well in every way, playing with other children. Before midday in the fields he suddenly fell down, speaking and acting as a demon and not able to see clearly. In half a month he was blind. On the sixth of the third month a native doctor, according to their ignorant practices, stuck needles in the inner corners of the eyes. On the thirteenth of that month the child was brought to the Christians. The demonism was healed by them, but the eye trouble persisted. When I first saw him, shortly after that, the eyes showed very slight symptoms of inflammation, the pupils were not clearly distinguishable in either eye and when I could slightly detect them, they showed a lead-bluish color. In May 1920, I saw the child. In the right eye the iris was now clearly defined and a good normal color.

There was a white spot, clearly marked. It was not on the cornea but back in the lens. It was smaller than the pupil and instead of being circular, it had an irregular jagged outline. The left eye was blurred, bluish-white and the pupil not clearly distinguishable. No contractions could be gotten. The patient did not look so hopelessly despondent as before and to inquiry replied that things looked 'variegated,' but he could not make out forms. The family gave up hope, would not accept Christianity, would not let the boy be sent to Shanghai, and he was not cured.

No. 38 was demonized about 1906 or '07, and blindness came on. She says there was never any 'eye disease.' In 1912 the Christians healed the demonism. When I first saw her, in 1919, she was normal in every way except being blind. The pupils were inflated and of a dull, muddy color. Iris and pupil were clearly defined. The lids moved freely. In March, 1920, J. W. Hewett, m.r.c.s., i,.r.c.p., diagnosed the case as atrophy of the optic nerves, primary, IE, coming on without inflammation. So far as he could judge after these years, he thought it may have been due to (1) mental strain, and (2) insufficient nourishment. The husband had taken a second wife and mistreated this one.

No. 349 is a woman thirty-seven years of age. In 1918, sixth month (about July), one day in the fields she began to laugh abnormally. They sent for the landlord. From that time on she had spells of demonism, coming off and on, and lasting three or four days. She would have pain in the head and the right eye. There was no trouble in the other eye. The right eye would become blurred so that she could not see the road. It got red and inflamed. She herself, the husband, and the landlord say the eye trouble came after the demonism. In the eighth month she was brought to the Christians and healed of the demonism. May 19, 1919, I saw her. She seemed entirely well, color good, flesh normal. The only symptom noticeable was that one eye would drip.

The tears did not come in a flow, nor were the eyes inflamed. I would see a single tear form and drop, then another and so on. I gave no drugs. In May, 1920, I saw her again, entirely well, even the eye. No. 79, after ten odd years of demonism, has the eyes inflamed. Now they have not healed entirely. although the demonism is healed, but are much better, No. 6 was a case of demonism with diarrhea, etc. When the demon came on usually at night, the patient's eyes became blurred. When the demonism was healed, the eyes also became normal. Miss Johnston's case, No. 122, was affected in the eye, when the demonism would come on.

It is evident that eye troubles cannot account for demonism, as only a beggar's dozen of the demon cases show affections of the eye. That they may predispose to demonism is possible. It may be that in these cases there were incipient eye troubles not noticed by parents and friends. But these data raise the interesting scientific problem, whether the converse may be true and hysteria can cause organic eye trouble. C. Lloyd Tuckey in his 'Treatment by Hypnotism and Suggestion' p.20, quotes Dr. James Reynolds to show that in some cases of hysteria, when the stimulus of the will has been long withheld, the nutrition of the nerves is impaired and a functional becomes an organic malady. In the 'Journal of Abnormal Psychology,' December 1919, Solomon Meyer takes issue with Tuckey on the ground that mere ideation cannot affect peripheral processes unless the emotional element comes into play. From the cases in the text it would seem that demonism can cause organic eye troubles, whether along the lines suggested by Reynolds or whether by the fear of demons acting as an emotive impulse. As to this whole question of etiology, we may conclude that physical factors of varying kinds may be looked for. Take, EG, No. 305. In the autumn of 1918, friends brought this man to the Christian chapel.

He had the appearance of one almost dead. Could not eat. Had violent spells of demonism. The Christians prayed with him. He began to eat and the demonism passed off. But after a time it was found that he did not urinate properly. In May 1919, he came to the hospital at Yeucheng, was circumcised and treated for gonorrhea. He is now normal. In No. 101, the ether used by Dr. Woods may have predisposed to demonism, but Americans never become demonized from ether. Such factors cannot be the efficient cause of demonism. If they were, New York would have as much demonism as Yencheng. Indeed the variety of the physical factors show they are merely excitatory. Local conditions in China show nothing of a physiological nature that could account for demonism. True, the opium habit is more prevalent here. But of all the cases I have observed only No. 1 was known to have used opium, and most of the cases are known not to have used it. As for nerves, the Chinese are proverbially stolid. Certainly one would be more likely to find hysterical temperaments among high-strung Westerners than among the Chinese. Nor can sexualism account for demonism. If so, there are places in our Western cities where demons would be as thick as blackberries on a bush. Indeed, in China it is not in the notoriously salacious places, like Soochow Road, Shanghai, that demonism is found, but in the retired country villages, where unchastity is comparatively rare. We may as well give up the idea that pathological science can explain demonism. The problem is chiefly one of psychics.

DEMONISM

CHAPTER V

Demonism Based on Perversion of Religion

To work out this psychic problem we must take our point of departure from the one outstanding characteristic of the trouble. It is based on perversion of the religious in man, on superstition. Man has and has always had religious impulses- some do not recognize them as instinctive- which lead to religious beliefs and practices. When such impulses, beliefs, practices are manifested in crude and superstitious forms, they result, as we shall see below, in these psychic abnormalities.

What is religion? Freud and others make it a matter of sublimation. They conceive of a current, a flow of biological, creative energy, which they call the libido. In lower forms of life it manifests itself in elemental impulses which make for life preservation and perpetuation of species. With evolutionary development the libido, as White says, "is ever striving to free itself from its limitations, to go onward and upward, to create, and in order to do this it must overcome resistances, tear loose from drag-backs, emancipate itself from the inertia of lower callings. The energy which succeeds is sublimated, refined, spiritualized." According to this view, as the libido, which would have fastened itself on lower ideals, sexual or otherwise, reaches out towards the higher, the ideals of majesty, power, fatherhood attract it, and the lower concepts are transposed, sublimated into the higher concept God. Jung, following out this thought, makes religion a biological product and necessary to biological development. It is not our place here to discuss on general grounds the question whether religion be objective or subjective; whether God made man, or man by subconscious processes evolved the god-idea. Religion is a fact, a biological fact, a historical fact. This fact is a safe starting-point for our

51

investigations. The form of religion which underlies modern civilization is the monotheistic, and we shall assume monotheism as the consensus of human thought on the subject of religion.

To make progress it is necessary that we first delimit superstition, science, religion. Superstition is a term constantly used, yet rarely defined. The dictionaries give various usages of the word, the sense being more or less dependent on the opinions of those using it. What may be, perhaps, the central meaning of the term pertains to the causation of phenomena in nature. In times past men peopled the air with spirits, free from the laws of cause and effect and superior thereto. When events occurred for which no cause was apparent, men guessed at causation by the interference of spirits. As a rebound from this, some would consider all belief in spiritualities as superstition. Others would apply the term to polytheism as distinguished from monotheism. A safe definition may be stated thus: Superstition is the ERRONEOUS ATTRIBUTING OP PHENOMENA IN NATURE TO DIRECT ARBITRARY VOLITION BY SPIRITS, TO THE DENIAL OR EXCLUSION OF SCIENTIFIC PRINCIPLES.

Science- using this term in the ordinary sense has made no generally accepted dictum as to the existence or otherwise of spiritualities. It has formulated no comprehensive theory of the cosmos, its origin, its government, its limitations. Science concerns itself only with matters which are considered susceptible of proof by demonstration, with the principles of natural law. Religion, what we may call normal religion, scientific religion, is at one with science in fully recognizing natural law, but it goes further and postulates a Supreme Intelligence, the source of all that is good, of all that makes for the highest development, physically, mentally, spiritually, of the universe, man included. God, as thus viewed, does not arbitrarily interfere with nature's laws. He has the power and the right, if occasion arises, to alter, to amend, to suspend, to destroy his creation, even as the master-mechanician still remains master of the clock, the engine, the gun he has made. But ordinarily the volition of the Divine operates through natural law. It embraces the disposing of forces, the working through agencies and means, the manipulating of this vast machine in such way as to give effective and continuous control of every part.

According to the monotheistic conception, whatever tends to resist the sovereignty of God, to violate nature's laws, either is morally evil or originates in the morally evil. Such evil is usually traced to a source, to the Spirit of Rebellion against the Divine embodied in the concept Satan. Thus light, knowledge, truth, health, the normal, what ought to be, are attributed to God. Ignorance, superstition, vice, falsehood, physiological and psychological deterioration are attributed, directly or indirectly, to Satan.

This epitome represents what may be considered the consensus of leading monotheistic thinkers and is in accordance with the teachings of the Old and New Testament. (Ex. 15:26; 23:25; Deut. 28:60; Ps. 103:3; Luke 10:17; Cor. 12:7.)

The application is, of course, on broad lines. No one would say that monotheists are free from ignorance and disease nor that polytheists or unbelievers have not health and knowledge. In a field of wheat on good soil, tended carefully and scientifically, nature's laws. IE, God's laws, apply more fully. Some of the wheat may, indeed, suffer in one way or another, but that does not alter the fact that it is a superior field of wheat. Another field, where soil is defective, culture neglected, may have some good wheat, but in the main it grows rank with weeds. In countries where enlightened forms of Christianity prevail, where scientific principles are better understood and more fully applied, where men live on a moral and cultured plane, man is generally superior, morally, intellectually and physically, than in other lands. As the Divine law is put into force more fully, there is cleansing from physical diseases originating in ignorance and sin. Our hospitals in the Orient abundantly witness to this fact. Also we are now discovering that psychic maladies are relieved by applying the principles of science and enlightened religion. It is in this sense that I call the highest form of monotheism, Christianity, normal religion. It makes for normal, right conditions.

Now the striking fact about demonism is that it does not occur, to any noticeable extent, where this normal religion, Christianity, prevails. Belief in God does not cause demonism. Nor is it caused by belief in the existence of non-corporeal entities other than God, good or bad. But wherever men worship or fear such spiritualities and demons, there we have demonism. It occurs where monotheism has not outgrown this superstitious fear of demons. Miss Janet Hay Houston writes from Mexico that in one of her meetings a woman rather deficient intellectually was seized with what appeared to be epilepsy. It occurred several times afterwards. Miss Houston noticed that it always occurred at the most vital part of the discourse. She recognized it as demonism and by the exercise of faith it was stopped.

Demonism is the natural, the logical outcome of polytheism, whether the spirits worshiped be Christian saints or 'heathen' demons. Demon worship is unscientific, abnormal. It antagonizes the sovereignty of the Divine and the rule of divine law, which is natural law. It is what I call mis-religion. It leads to perverted concepts, to a crouching, cringing spirit of readiness to worship anything from the God of Heaven to the gods of grasshoppers and of the kitchen range. The vicious tendency of polytheism is not determined by the moral quality of the concept worshiped, nor even by its existence. The term demon' in its primary significance, the classic Greek 'daimon' and the Chinese 'kwei,' had no moral significance. A demon in this sense might be a mythological concept, a departed hero, a saint, just as well as a diabolical demon. Thus when Paul and John spoke of the worship of demons, they were referring to the Corinthian and other gods, many of whom represented departed human beings, whom they considered saints. He also called the Athenians 'demon apprehensive' (Acts 17: 22). They seemed to accept his appellation and wanted to know whether Jesus was another 'demon' for them to worship. The fundamental idea of the term 'demon' was non-corporeality. It shows out in Ignatius' version of Jesus' remark after his resurrection: "I am not a demon without a body," *ouk eimi daimonion asomaton*. (Luke 24: 39).

The morally evil element in polytheism is in the rebellion against nature and nature's ruler. This throws it in line with the Satan principle- evil, antagonism to law, antagonism to the good, antagonism to God, as monotheistically conceived. The demonism resulting from this demon-worship was characteristically evil. Thus the secondary sense of the term, which the New Testament Greek differentiated by the form 'daimon' or by adding an adjective to 'daimonion,' soon fixed itself on language and superseded the primary.

Now for the proof of what we have been laying down. That demonism originates in superstition we shall see: I. From the history of demonism in the past, II. From the conditions in which it now prevails. III. From the facts manifested in the cases we have observed.

I. Before the Christian era polytheists worshiped, and monotheists feared demons, and Josephus tells us that demonism prevailed at least as far back as Solomon's times. The Christ had to contend with it. Under the primitive forms of Christianity it continued. Indeed epidemics have occurred in comparatively modern times, but only where the fear of demons prevailed. One such was at Morzinnes, Upper Savoy, in 1857. The demonism seen there was similar to what we are discussing, but was sporadic and the hysterical convulsion was a more marked feature. Whether or not the witchcraft of the past was demonism we have not clear data. Much, e.g., of the Salem witchcraft was deviltry by human demons, as one sees by reading Cotton Mather's 'Wonders of the Invisible World.' But New England was settled in the times of James I, whose book 'Daemonologie' gave royal support to current absurdities. The environment was certainly such as we see does produce demonism. Among the negroes of America there may occur demonism, though much of their conjuring was mere fraud.

II. In modern times, under enlightened Christian conditions, demonism is certainly not prevalent, and proof has yet to be brought of its existence. The case of Gottleib in Dittus in Germany, is no exception, for in all probability there was local fear of demons. Several cases of supposed demonism in America have been reported to me, but on inquiry they seemed to resemble the insanities. The demonism of today is found to be co-extensive with practically all lands except those under enlightened forms of Christianity. It is reported from all parts of China, from India, Africa, Japan, Korea, Moslem lands, the South Sea Islands. As to Japan, Chamberlain in his 'Things Japanese' gives a quotation from Dr. Baelz as follows: "Possession by foxes is a form of nervous disorder or delusion not uncommonly observed in Japan. Having entered a human being... the fox lives a life of his own apart from the proper self of the person who is harboring him. The person possessed hears and understands everything the fox inside says or thinks, and the two often engage in a loud and angry dispute, the fox speaking in a voice altogether different from that which is natural to the individual... Among the predisposing conditions may be mentioned a weak intellect, a superstitious turn of mind, and such debilitating diseases as typhoid fever. Possession never occurs except in such subjects as have heard of it already and believe in the reality of its existence."

In 'The Moslem World,' July 1913, Miss Anna Y. Thompson and Miss Elisabet Franke report demonism in Moslem lauds. While Mohammedanism recognizes only the worship of Allah, yet the demons are feared. Indeed in the 'zars,' the exorcisms, there is burning of candles and sweets to please the spirits, and there is sacrifice of sheep and fowls. These are essentially forms of worship.

In the Journal of the North China Branch of the Royal Asiatic Society (1918), Dr. Zwemer brings out the Moslem's fear of demons. On waking he blows his nose three times because demons inhabit the nostrils in sleep. Constant washings are required to get rid of demons, care being taken lest they hide between the fingers. Yawning and sneezing are attributed to demonic origin, and prayer or ejaculation is necessary to remove such influences. As to Africa, Dr. J. L. Wilson says: "Demoniacal possessions are common and the feats performed by those supposed to be under such influences are certainly not unlike those described in the New Testament. Frantic gestures, convulsions, foaming at the mouth, feats of supernatural strength, furious ravings, bodily lacerations, gnashing of teeth and other things of similar character, may be witnessed in most of the cases."

Rt. Rev. Frank Weston, D.D., Bishop of Zanzibar, in his 'The Christ and His Critics', gives testimony to actual experience with demonism in his field. Canon Arthur F. Williams in our Nos. 145 to 150 gives ample proof of demonism in New Zealand. He also confirms Dr. Wilson's testimony about Africa, giving as his authority a medical man, formerly in Africa, but now living in New Zealand.

III. That demonism is to be traced to idolatry will be seen by a careful reading of my data. No. 2 was a clear case of demonism originating in fear of the weasel spirit which they worship. A weasel had been brought to her village, and several persons were affected through their fears of this demon. In No. 67 that superstition was the prime factor is evidenced by the fact that this woman had for twenty years carefully preserved the old idol worshiping it faithfully, and whenever she relaxed diligence in burning incense the spells would come on. When the idol was taken down, she was healed. Take my case No. 73, a bright schoolboy. His father had accepted Christianity and the uncle had been baptized. In obedience to the urgings of the grandfather, still an idolater, the father, against his own judgment, again burnt incense. Soon afterwards they were repairing the home and took down the fox idol. Two or three days later, just after supper, this boy was sitting by the table, resting his head upon it. All of a sudden, without provocation, he became wild, threw his arms and legs around and talked in the personality of the fox god.

The Christians were sent for. They held worship. Ere long the boy joined in the singing and in a day or two was well. He has had no trouble since, and when I have seen him on many occasions he always seemed normal. No. 97, another young boy, was taken when he joined an idol procession. In No. 58, the trouble originated with the worship of the fox god by the grandmother of the patient's husband.

That demonism originates with the worship of idols is evidenced by the fact that the demons usually speak in the personality of the idols worshiped, and demand the burning of incense. In some cases, temporary relief may be purchased by yielding to such demands. Thus No. 108, the supposed case of tetanus, was relieved as soon as the promise was made to burn incense. Practically all on the mission field who have come in contact with these cases testify that they can be cured only on condition of giving up the idolatry. In cases which we have failed to cure, we usually find that an idol has been hidden under the bed or somewhere.

Take my No. 25. Trouble began with his father, who was a wizard and robber besides. He had a little idol about a foot long. Christians persuaded him to give up the idol and quit practicing witchcraft. Not long afterwards he died. The wife and the son were convinced that the demon had caused the death, so a duplicate of the idol was made. Shortly afterwards the boy's young wife was afflicted (No. 3). Her brother was a Christian man, and while visiting in his home she was healed by prayer and much effort on his part. Immediately her husband, this No. 25, a hearty young farmer, became afflicted, and has been so for several years. At any time of day or night he will begin to talk as the demon. He talks and chants much like the father and the wife did. He feels the demon holding him down. When an attack comes on in sleep the family wake him and it gradually passes off. On November 30, 1918, his brother-in-law and a Christian tried to persuade him to give up the idol. He told them that on account of the mother he had to leave it up, but would himself not worship it. That day he came before the session. I noticed decided nervousness, quick manner of speech, nervous laugh. He was not cured and since that has not dared to come to the session.

No. 109 is a case in point. Miss King reported that she had known this woman for fifteen years, and had often seen her, both when under the influence and when not so. The woman said that she was wretched, that she longed to be delivered but could not. When Miss King talked to her of Jesus the woman cursed her, but apologized for it afterwards, when the influence was passed. Once she threw water on Miss King in the same way. When speaking as the demon the voice was changed and the eye abnormal. She practiced witchcraft.

Two years before Miss King's first report (in Dec. 1915) the patient tried to give up idolatry, but still left the idols up. Soon afterwards the arm with which she used to burn incense was paralyzed. The leg was not affected nor the mind, so far as reported. By yielding to the idols, the trouble passed off, but she was in bondage and deeply troubled. In January 1916, she made up her mind definitely and burned the idols. On several occasions since that date Miss King has reported her well. We may thus safely lay down the principle that demonism is rooted in perverted religious beliefs and practices. Now, why should polytheism produce demonism and Christianity cure it? This question we shall try to work out in later chapters.

CHAPTER VI

Principles on which the mind can be demonized

We are bearing towards the crux of our problem: Can demonism be accounted for without outside influence? We now see that superstition or perversion of the religious nature of man is the immediate agency, the connecting wire, so to speak. But to reach our problem we must first find out on what scientific principles this superstition works.

In the rapid advance of scientific investigation into diseases of psychic origin, several schools of thought have arisen, all of them holding more or less of the truth. I. Dubois traced the origin of many diseases to perverted mental states. He wrote, e.g." People are only what they can be by virtue of the mentality with which they were endowed and the education which they have received." His treatment was based on the idea of bringing men to think and act according to reason. Certain classes of investigators have worked along the lines of psycho-analysis. Their method is to analyze the workings of the subconscious mind and find therein psychic conditions which have been causing ailments, psychological and pathological. The Freudian system finds psychic disturbances arising from the repression by the conscious mind of sexual experiences of the past, which had taken refuge, as it were, in the subconscious, and there wrought out friction unseen. Especial emphasis is laid on infantile perversions of a sexual nature, hidden from parent and nurse. It was Freud's dictum that "no neurosis is possible in a normal vita sexualis." Jung, taking the general principles of psychanalysis, finds Freud's hypothesis of a past, and often an infantile experience making a permanent, determining, dominating impression on the whole life insufficiently supported. He also puts the trouble in the subconscious, but in the present rather than the past. His system is based largely on the idea of the libido. By this term psycho-analysts signify the current of biological energy, flowing through the whole life.

It is conceived of subjectively and consciously as desire, and manifests itself first in the infant suckling, later in sexual desire, later still as religion, and so on through the life with all its manifold cravings. This libido, according to Jung, meets an obstruction. Environmental conditions present an obstacle. The libido endeavors to overcome it. Failing that, there is a 'regression.' The subconscious mind seeks an outlet for this libido in some primitive or abnormal form of gratification, whether sexual or otherwise. Adlerism is another phase of psycho-analysis. One phase of it especially concerns us. In the human being are organs and functions more or less plastic and adaptable. The libido aims to establish a well-balanced harmony. When an organ or function is defective, the libido can, to a greater or less extent, remedy the defect by the law of compensation. We see this in a simpler way thus. When a nerve is injured, another nerve can take up its work. When one-half of the brain is injured, under some circumstances the other half can be brought into play and can take up its work.

According to Adler, defect in some organ or function may work out psychologically in character formation and in the psychic life generally. This adjusting is the work of the nervous system and the brain. It is, as Adler sees it, in the failure of the brain to establish a compensatory system, satisfying the demands of the libido, that nervous troubles arise. Prince and other students of abnormal psychology interpret many psychopathic conditions, including dissociation of personality, as caused by the impulsive dynamic force of the emotions. Intense emotional impulses, says he, intensify certain activities and inhibit others. Hence arises conflict. In this way systematized groups of ideas with emotional tones may become dissociated and operate as distinct personalities. In the conflict both conscious and unconscious states may be concerned, or in some cases the dissociation may be effected by entirely subconscious processes.

Sidis attributes psychopathic conditions to the waste of nerve energy, the using up of what he calls dynamic energy- that which operates in normal life- and the drawing on reserve energy. As the dynamic and reserve energy is used up, psychopathic disturbances arise, emotional impulses become more violent, there is reversion to lower forms of mental activity, neuropathic conditions succeed the psychopathic, and as what he calls the static and the organic nerve energies are drawn on, the nerve cells are affected and disintegration takes place, ending in the death of the nerve tissue. The waste of nerve energy he lays to the door of the fear impulse based on the biological instinct for the preservation of life. Sidis does not limit psychic perversions to the subconscious.

In these several systems there are similarities and diversities. In all of them prominence is given to the subconscious, to the wish, to environment, to maladjustment, to psychic conflict. Some or all of these principles have their part to play in demonism as we shall see, but no one of them alone can find the solution of our fundamental question: What causes this form of dissociation?

Let us say with Dubois that it comes from the slavery of peoples to their innate and acquired mentality. That is most true, but let us be more specific. On what principle can this perverted mental state, the fear of demons, lead to demonism? Freud could probably find some father complexes and mother complexes among the Chinese, but why should such things in China produce demonism while in the West they produce insanities and nervous diseases? Infantile sexual perversions are not more common in China than in the West, if as much so. For twenty seven years I have observed the naked children of China and can remember only two or three instances in which I have seen erotic manifestations. Some of our cases are influenced by Jung's principles. I believe he solves for us the problem as to why the poor daughters-in-law are so liable to this trouble.

Only a few days ago I was examining No. 406. Her husband, telling how his mother had been demonized for thirty or forty years, practicing witchcraft and breaking out in demon talk almost any time, remarked that his wife also was afflicted. When I asked the wife herself, she replied that in her maiden home she had never been troubled but that as soon as she came into this home the demon had taken her and she had been afflicted several years. So also said Nos. 58, 386, and many others. These girls leave their old homes and come into new environment under the domination of a Chinese mother-in-law, the last word in autocracy. They can do nothing, but must think. Their libido has met an obstruction. Their thoughts, forgotten it may be, go down into the unconscious and make them fit subjects for dissociation. But as to our problem, ask Jung: Why does maladjustment to environment produce demonism in China and not in the West? You will see the most essential factor has not been brought out. So, also, with Adlerism. In the West the libido striving to work out compensation for an inferior organ or function, may lead to hosts of psychoses and neuroses, but not to demonism. Why should it do so in the East?

As to Sidis's principle, in Western lands there is fear, fear of God, fear of demons. This combines with indifferent stimuli, exhausts the nerve energy, and leads to phobias, to paranoias, to catatonic precox, to hysteric and neurasthenic conditions, but not to demonism.

As to psychic conflict, in some instances of demonism

DEMONISM

we find indications of it as a predisposing factor. But my observation is that conflict leads rather to the insanities than to demonism proper. Take my No. 93. In a family there developed friction between three brothers over the division of the property. The younger of the three was then, October, 1917, an inquirer. He began to show abnormal excitement, was troubled with insomnia, his face would flush.

He would button-hole people anywhere and everywhere, demanding, Do you know Jesus? He began to have spells of raving. The voice would become unnatural. This continued off and on for several months, until our people cured him. Now insomnia is characteristic of the insanities, but not particularly so of demonism. There was no clear record of either dissociation or control. The excitement, the over- religiosity sound more like manic-depressive insanity than demonism.

No. 8 is another case in point. The wife of this man was of a well-to-do family and he not poor. But they had no child. If he should die, the property would go to his brothers. In 1914 he began to be afflicted with what was supposed to be a demon. Spells would come on. He would lie down for three or four days, neither eating nor drinking. So intense was their anxiety to see him healed that the wife, on one occasion, with ignorant loyalty, cut out a piece of her own arm for him to eat, thinking thus to restore him. On Dec. 31, 1918, he was shown to me. He was thin and husky, with a cough, possibly tubercular. Now this case seems to have arisen from the conflict. But there is no record of dissociation nor of control. He did not yield to the treatment, as so many of the demonized do, and that though he asked for prayer and indeed prayed himself. Death resulted about a month afterwards. This seems more like disease, mental or physical, or both.

An attractive hypothesis is that demonism arises from

the impact of Christianity on other religious systems. The theory is based in part on the erroneous idea that the demonism in Jesus' time was due to his attacks on the old Jewish religion. Some Bible students make the same mistake, though they express it differently. Judging from the apparent absence of demonism in the Old Testament times, they say that in the times of the Christ, the demons came forth specially to combat him.

A closer reading of the Bible explodes these ideas. The exorcists to whom Christ referred were evidently a well-known class of men with practices coming down from the ages of the past. Josephus throws light on the subject. There were in his day well-known remedies for demonism, which he believed to have come down from the time of Solomon. In his 'Wars with the Jews,' he discourses on the root baaras supposed to heal it, and states the established belief that the demons were spirits of the dead come back to worry people. His narrative paralleling 2 Kings it shows that the discussions about Beelzebub in the time of Christ arose from a custom as old as the times of Elijah of going to Baalzebub- the older form of the name- the 'Fly,' god of to cure maladies attributed to demons.

In 'Antiquities' he shows from a discourse which he attributes to Jonathan, based of course on Jewish opinion and probably on ancient documents, that the 'evil spirit' which afflicted Saul was a demon and was exorcised by David. Expositors have fought shy of this interpretation because it would give them a nut to crack. How could Jehovah send a demon on Saul? Having enough nuts of my own to crack, I shall not attempt this one. Suffice it to say that this statement is on a par with that other one, 'Jehovah hardened Pharaoh's heart.'

The Scripture record is illuminated by this Jewish view that Saul was demonized. We can now see how at one minute he could be loving David and making him his son-in-law, but in a

DEMONISM

flash he would be in a passion, throwing a javelin at him- this was the demon's doings. That demonism far antedated the Christ is brought out by the Encyclopedia Britannica, Ninth Edition, by Tylor's 'Primitive Culture,' and by other authorities. Turning now to China we find that demonism cannot be due to the conflict between Christianity and other religions. It has prevailed from all past times. The Tso Chiien, one of the Chinese classics, written certainly before B.C. 206, has the famous passage known to scholars by the odd phrase, Kao ts'i slicing mang ts'i ksia. The Marquis of Chin dreamed of a demon. A wizard warned him not to eat the new wheat. In a second dream he saw two boys (demons) discoursing as to whether the famous physician who had been called could oust them.

One said that as they were situated above the kao, an organ in the region of the heart, and below the mang, which Giles translates 'throat,' he could not hurt them. On arriving, the physician said that very thing, that the trouble was above the kao, and below the mang, so that he could not reach it, whether with needles or with drugs. The Marquis rewarded the physician, killed the wizard, ate the new wheat and immediately swelled and died. The data reported are not sufficient for us to diagnose whether this was demonism or disease or both. The author and the famous physician believed it to be demonism, and the case reflects conditions in those times.

The 'Annals of the Later Divided Kingdoms of the Han Dynasty' is one of the established historical works of China, written in the Chin Dynasty, before A.D. 419.

The exposition of these annals* gives the following record: "A Prince named Swen Ch'iien killed Kwan Yiiin Ch'ang and took his territory. In the feast of celebration Swen was praising one of his leaders named Lii Meng, and pouring wine, handed it to him. Lii Meng took the wine and was about to drink.

DEMONISM

Suddenly He threw down the cup, gripped his own prince Swen and cursed him violently: 'You green-eyed bristly rat, do you know me?' The terrified courtiers tried to defend their prince, but Lii threw him down and with a great stride sat on his throne. His eyebrows stuck out. Both eyes were distended like suns. With a loud voice he said: 'From the time I went out to subdue the Yellow Turban brigands I ran things for thirty years. By intrigue you have ruined me. While alive I could not overcome you, but now dead I must seize your soul. I am Kwan Yiiin Ch'ang.' With that Lii Meng fell prone on the floor, blood flowing from the seven apertures, and died."

Now this story may be mere superstitious babble. But the record is from a history fully as well established as Thucydides, Xenophon, Tacitus. However we may interpret it, there is ample analogy in records of to-day for enabling us to receive as fact such a record of a courtier becoming dissociated, assuming the personality of a dead enemy, as such assaulting his prince, and himself dying under the experience. We may take further testimony from a reputable pharmacopeia, generally used by Chinese doctors and officially sanctioned (The 'Pen Ts'ao Kang Moh'). It was written in the time of the Manchu Emperor, Swen Chih, A. D. 1644. In Vol. XII, under 'Herbs, tractylis ovata, history of the plant' we read: "The encyclopedias say that in Chehkiang Province a married woman named Kao had a disease. She would speak abnormally. The spirit of her dead husband possessed her. The family burnt this plant and the demon immediately sought to leave her." Here follows also the case of a Kiaugsi scholar demonized. These cases are selected from reliable works. Volumes could be filled from those of less repute. But Christianity made no considerable impression on China until the time of Kanghsi, A. D. 1662, later than any of these cases.

From the above it is clear that demonism prevailed widely in ages before Christ came, and continued in the past for centuries before Christianity was heard of. It is impossible, therefore, to account for it on the ground of psychic conflict arising from the antagonism of the old and the new religions.

With this, as with other forms of psychic conflict, the tendency is strongly towards the insanities rather than demonisin. No. 133 is a case in point. This was plainly manic-depressive insanity, and was so diagnosed by Dr. Nelson Bell. Mrs. J. R. Graham saw an attack- the first one so far as the manifestations were reported. The patient, a woman, suddenly sprang up and began to jump three feet high, whirling around as she jumped. She now talked very rapidly and chanted three word phrases. She believed herself under the control of something, she knew not whether god or a demon. It became necessary to chain her and she was sent thus to the mission hospital. After being released, she struck Dr. Bell with the chain and had to be chained up again. She improved under treatment, but did not entirely recover and was taken away.

This case may be clearly traced to the conflict of religions. She had been a Taoist devotee of unusual devotion and had attained a Taoist rank almost equal to canonization. She lived in an idolatrous widow's home, to which ordinarily neither Chinese men nor missionaries were admitted. There is no report of trouble before the missionaries were invited there to treat a disease. Her conception of control was not expressed in idolatrous phraseology as that of a fox or a weasel demon. She came gradually to speak of 'The True God' controlling her, using a distinctively Christian term. This is a typical case of how the conflict of religions may affect a nervous system in a personality not properly broadened and harmonized. A mind with an intense devotion, isolated from all contact with the outside world, mulling in its own little round of thought, suddenly gets a new idea with a powerful emotive stimulus, and is thrown out of balance. Conflict is the dominating factor in many of the insanities, but with demonism another factor is even more prominent.

The principle on which superstition leads to demonism is the Law of Suggestion. All schools of psychiatry recognize and use this principle. We shall see below that Prince's emotive impulse and Sidis's nerve exhaustion bear strongly on this phase of our subject. But first, for the sake of the uninformed, I must show what science means by suggestion and that it is the predominating causative factor.

The Law of Suggestion is the principle on which science interprets the phenomena of mesmerism, hypnotism, mental healing and the like. The general public have always been shy of this subject. It looks uncanny. Hence poor Mesmer died in poverty and exile, while Braid, to whom we owe the term hypnotism, had his life embittered by social ostracism. Science owes much to such men, even though it discards many of their theories. Mesmer held that in 'mesmerizing' people the operator exercised power over them, that from him emanated what he called 'animal magnetism,' and it was this which influenced the subject. Braid interpreted the matter along physiological lines. In his day psychiatry was not developed. One of his methods was to have the subject look fixedly at a bright light. Hypnotism would result. Modern psychiatry, working on the principle of suggestion, also uses some physical means, but they are subsidiary.

Science holds that hypnotization is an automatic reaction on the part of the subject; that under proper conditions a suggestion is received by the subject and he automatically hypnotizes himself. To illustrate, at the sight of food, one becomes hungry; on going into a dark room, the pupils dilate. These are both automatic reactions of the nervous system. In hypnotizing a subject, the operator is the directing mind, and causes the hypnotization, but he does not do so by exerting power, as Mesmer thought. What he really does is to stage the proper conditions- in which both psychic and physical methods may be brought into play- and then to inject into the mind of the subject the belief that he is being hypnotized. The subject's mind and nervous system react to this suggestion and hypnotization results.

We have seen that demooism is dissociation. But hypnotism is merely the old name for artificial dissociation. Hypnotism is now fully recognized and used by scientists of the first rank. The present knowledge of hysteria came largely through study and experiment by hypnotic methods. It was Charcot and the Paris School of psychiatrists who developed this study. The Nancy School took up the subject and carried it further, proving that hypnotism by suggestion may be used with the normal as well as with hysterics. The particular form of hysteria which we call dissociation of personality has been studied chiefly by hypnotic methods. Many of the well-known cases of dissociation were discovered by artificially hypnotizing hysterical patients.

Those who have studied demonism at first hand have generally recognized the element of suggestion in it. In dealing with the Morzinnes epidemic, M. Constans recognized it and in one case used hypnotism as a means of treatment.

In many, if not all, of my cases suggestion is evident. My Nos. 417 and 418 were what I call virgin cases. The witches sometimes tell a young girl that a spirit has transmigrated into her, who in the other world was a slave girl, under vows of perpetual virginity; hence that if she, the girl, gets married, she will certainly die. This terrible form of suggestion is all too fatal. Both of these two cases were so influenced. No. 418 had been ill, off and on, for two years, and whenever the family began preparations for her wedding, she would be taken with a spell. Under our ministry both of these cases seemed to be healed. With No. 417 preparations had already been going ahead for the funeral. But our people raised her up. Later reports, however, would indicate that they have probably again fallen under the power of the witches.

No. 141 was a demonized boy. Christians healed him, requiring the family to put away idolatry. But the mother, hesitating to destroy her god, gave it to a married sister. When the boy, later, saw it again in the sister's house, suggestion brought back his old trouble and he was down for a week. Then he was brought to Mrs. J. W. Paxton, looking very ill and speaking strangely. He was healed, but friends advised him to make his living by peddling an article used in idolatrous worship. This, too, had in it suggestion and another attack occurred. Only when finally rid of everything suggesting idolatry was he permanently healed. I saw him six months later, normal.

The whole train of thought in preceding chapters may be summarized as proof that suggestion underlies demonism. I. Demonism cannot be classed with the other insanities. II. It cannot be accounted for on merely pathological grounds. III. No other psychological principle can account for it independently of suggestion. IV. This hypothesis is based on well-established principles and is in line with the opinions of authorities. V. It allows for the demonizing of the healthy as well as of the pathological. VI. It accounts for all the kaleidoscopic symptoms. VII. It is consonant with the healing by psychic means alone.

This gives us a rational interpretation of this malady. The fear of demons brings the fixation of attention, the monotony of thought, the limiting of the field of consciousness, and other conditions which Sidis shows are necessary to hypnotization. A subject thus hypnotized follows out passively false suggestions

DEMONISM

inherent in ignorant mental concepts.

Take a subject hypnotized before an audience. The operator tells him he is a dog. Had he never seen a dog, he would not know what to do. But he has in his mind already the concept 'dog.' Immediately he gets on all fours, barks, bites. Now take a demon case. The subject believes himself to be under the control of the Fox God. There is no Fox God. He does not impersonate the biological concept of the fox. But there is in his mind the superstitious concept of the spirit fox and he automatically does what he believes that spirit would do. This is not imaginary, it is not feigned. It is a most real psycho-physical condition. It is abject bondage by this hypnotization of the mind to all the mass of superstition and folklore of these old countries.

Now let us return to the views of psychiatrists. We have traced demonism to the law of suggestion. Fear and psychic conflict without suggestion do not produce demonism. A sporadic case in Western lands like that of Gottleibin Dittus does not disprove, but confirms this position. Examination of such cases will show that there was belief that demons can possess men. But Prince shows f that suggestion itself, having the force of a volition or unexpressed wish, gives rise to emotive impulse and promotes conflict. We may thus recognize suggestion itself as the casus belli, so to speak. And Sidis has shown that 'the fear instinct and its offspring- anxiety... weaken, dissociate and paralyze the functions of body and mind."

We can see, then, how suggestion operates; intensifying emotive impulses, causing fear and anxiety, and thus making one liable to hypnotization. But note the word liable. Granting these environmental conditions, the prevalence of the fear, how comes it that some are demonized and some not? If this belief alone were the efficient cause of the demonism, all under these conditions would be demonized. Just so in Western lands, many are fit subjects for hypnotizing, but they are not hypnotized without a hypnotizing agent.

A still more fundamental question is, Whence comes this environment? By analyzing demonism as hypnotism we have by no means accounted for it on a subjective basis. We have merely found the modus, the scientific principles on which it operates.

The discovery of the law of gravitation did not account for the motions of the spheres. Deeper questions are yet before us.

CHAPTER VII

Satanic Origin of Demonism

In all ages, men have tried to disprove or laugh off the fact that the world has an enemy, Satan, who works against all that is good. The facts of demonism confirm the Bible on this point.

At this statement my readers will be variously affected according to their customary attitude of mind. The religious will read with avidity, the anti-religious will scoff. Scientists will endeavor to read without bias. But in conversation several expressed the view that belief in spiritualities should be accepted only as a last resort. This, too, is an unjustifiable bias. If the arguments for, outweigh those against the influence of spiritualities, to tip the scales with a materialistic doubt is not scientific impartiality.

Let us first get rid of a misconception, namely, that the advance of science, dispelling superstition, has disproved the existence of spiritualities. We need to analyze the situation. Belief in spirits- aside from Biblical and theological apologetica- has heretofore rested largely on phenomena apparently not explainable on scientific principles, leading to the hypothesis of causation by nonhuman agencies. Superstitious ideas about direct interference of spirits in the ordinary course of nature have long since been discredited. There yet remains what are called the occult phenomena. The general tendency of science is to attribute these to the subconscious powers on one or other of several hypotheses. The Societies for Psychic Research stand for the existence of human personalities after death and the possibility of their communicating with, and thus influencing men.

DEMONISM

Wallace and others of the earlier members interpreted all occult phenomena on the hypothesis of continuous spirit influence. Myers, in bringing out the principles of disintegrated, i.e, dissociated personalities, took the position that with living beings a dissociated personality could operate independently, thus accounting for these occult powers, which he designated as sensory automatisms, motor automatisms, etc. From this starting point he held that the recognition of such powers on the part of the living relieved the necessity of hypothesizing the continuous spirit influence and at the same time tended to the comprehension of the spirit world and a more rational conception thereof.

It is attempted to account for these occult phenomena on the theories of telepathy, clairvoyance, clairaudience, and the like, as powers of the normal integrated mind. Such theories are still tentative. Again, cautious science, afraid of either of these views, recognizes hyperesthesia, a faculty allowing for the extension to a limited degree of the perceptive powers of man. This faculty is, however, too limited to account for all the known phenomena. In demonism these occult powers occur. Case No. 124 lived ten miles from the city where the missionaries were. Her husband went for the Christians. In the meantime the patient, on her bed, began to tell just what the party were doing. "Now they have started. Now they are going along by such a street. Now they have stopped and taken off their hats. Now they are at the door." Thus she followed exactly their every movement, even to the stopping on the way for prayer. The interpreting of these occult phenomena as functions of human powers, whether subconscious or otherwise, does not antagonize, but rather strengthens the hypothesis that there are spiritualities. It does effectively disabuse the superstitious idea that spiritualities manipulate affairs without regard to scientific principles.

But if science can see principles on which it may be

possible to understand the influence of spiritualities, it gives a 'provisional intelligibility,' as Myers would say, that may lead in time to demonstrable proof. We see that a living human organism may form one or more secondary personalities, alternating with the primary. Prince shows us that a co-conscious secondary personality may be formed, as Sally was, early in life, incubate and grow unseen in the subconscious, having perceptions, memory, thoughts unknown to the primary. Myers would hold that such a secondary personality can function apart from the body. Certainly the functions attributed to the subconscious, whether or not formed into a co-conscious personality, are not unlike what religious writers attribute to the soul. If we can find out the workings of the soul in the living man, problems of the future look less incomprehensible. Science has not negatived the existence of spiritualities, but rather is feeling for light.

But I do not base my argument for the existence of Satan on these occult phenomena. We shall see, as we proceed, that the facts of demonism, as interpreted in terms of modern science, lead us to a Satan.

We have found that demonism is, as to origin, essentially hypnotic. In looking for the ultimate origin, our next step is to consider the two phases of the subject, auto- and volitional hypnotization, and the bearings of this on our problem. Let us keep in mind that all hypnotization is automatic. Given the necessary conditions- what some have called an attitude of 'expectant attention'- and a suggestion, the human organism automatically slips the bolt and unshifts itself. What is meant by the term 'auto-hypnotization' is that the conditions arise and a suggestion occurs accidentally, as we say, i.e., without known purpose.

My case No. 58, Mrs. Ts'wei, originated thus. The husband's grandmother used to be a witch, a devotee of the Fox

DEMONISM

Spirit and controlled by it. At her death the trouble came upon her daughter-in-law. At the death of this second Mrs. Ts'wei, it came upon her daughter-in-law, our No. 58. In a little village, remote from all broadening influences, bound down by the conviction of the supernatural powers of the fox, the attention riveted by anticipation due to the family history, the conditions had arisen, this No. 58's mind had seized a suggestion and a secondary personality had split off. The conditions necessary to hypnotization were inherent in the environment, and we may consider this auiohypnotization. Tracing demonism to auto-hypnotization does not, however, solve the problem as to its ultimate origin.

The question still faces us, Whence comes this environment? How is it that men worship foxes and mythical beings? How is it that they believe in the power of such spiritualities to 'possess' people? And the one question that persists is, Whence comes the evil quality in demonism?

The question as to origin of the environment and of the evil quality in this environment resolves itself into two questions, Is there First Cause in general ? And, Is there a First Cause of Evil? We will now discuss the first of these questions. Are second causes adequate to account for the universe? The law of cause and effect is wide-reaching in the psychological as well as the physiological spheres. The disposing of conditions which lead to environmental suggestion and prepare a mind to receive it automatically may be considered but links in the chain of cause and effect. Even the human will is influenced by heredity, education, etc. The judgments, emotions, purposes of the Anglo-Saxon would be impossible in the Hottentot or the Malay, at least without bringing them under the environmental influences that have prevailed in civilized lands.

Even the ethical may be influenced by this law. Factors

psychic and factors physical may affect moral, indeed religious phenomena. Structure of the brain, heredity, disease, may have much to do with whether a man is morally good or morally evil. In these causes the psychic and the physical mutually interact. Scientists of a type now passing away, when they touched the border line of physiology and psychology, came to a halt. But modern investigators are losing sight of this line. Adolf Meyer speaks of the 'medically useless contrast of mental and physical.' Scientists now trace psychic effects to physical causes, and with almost equal facility, physical effects to psychic causes. Defects in the brain, causing psychic abnormalities, may be traced back to sin and ignorance in earlier links of the chain.

Yet, after all, the cause and effect principle itself presupposes a cause. The steam engine is a piece of mechanism based on the expansive power of heat. But the law of heat expansion could never have made a steam engine. The law of gravitation makes water run down a hill, but this law could never have made the water nor the hill, nor put them together. Scientific laws are themselves dead, mechanical principles. They cannot even manipulate themselves, so as to make an engine or a stream of water. How much less could they have created themselves and all things.

The law of cause and effect gives a working hypothesis as to the modus of phenomena; but the human mind refuses to be satisfied with any philosophy which leaves the cosmos as a mechanical automaton, a vast machine, self-created, self-starting, self-running, with no dynamic, no governing mentality behind it. Furthermore, biological evolution, when it leaves ultimate cause out of the equation, try as it will, cannot account for the noblest ideals of man, especially self sacrifice, altruism. Its principles are essentially and necessarily self-centric. It is based on the survival of the fittest, the right of the stronger to live at the expense of the weaker. Darwinianism unmodified, leads logically and actually to Prussianism- the right of might- and aspires to the superman as the next step in evolution. It has been attempted to account for altruism by saying that nature empirically finds the advantages of self-sacrifice for the common good, and thus has developed this principle. This lowers ethics to utilitarianism and emasculates nobility. It accounts for nobility by denying its existence! Again it has been attempted to interpret self-sacrifice on the principle of over functioning, that the ethical is a biological, useful apparatus and self destruction is the abnormal functioning of this principle. Then self-sacrifice becomes an abnormality, a psychic excrescence. This cannot be accepted.

There is in man enough of God to prove that God is. A Divine ultimate cause is an inevitable hypothesis. Let us look at this from another viewpoint, namely, the relation between freedom and necessity. This is a battle ground famous both in theology and science. Religious thinkers have lined up behind Augustine and Calvin, or Pelagius and Arminius. Some scientists advocate a determinism which would make a Calvinists hair stand on end. On the other hand Sir Oliver Lodge and Munsterberg, usually antagonists, both bring out the argument that the objective relations of man, the function of the faculties of a human personality, are servants; that there is a life which dominates these, and which cannot be subordinated to their control. Lodge says, e.g., "Terrestrial animals are all, in a sense, one family; and their hereditary links with the psychical universe consist of the physiological mechanism called brain and nerve. But these most interesting material structures are our servants, not our masters."

Munsterberg draws a distinction between the psycho-physiological realm of mechanical cause-and-effect relationships and what he calls the inner life, the true life; which consists, as he holds, of a succession of will-attitudes, which are free and dominating. Thus he says: "The real will is not a perceivable object, and therefore neither cause nor effect, but has its value and meaning in itself; it is not an exception to the world of laws and causes; no, there would not be any meaning in asking whether it has a cause or not, as only existing objects can belong to the series of causal relations. The real will is free, and it is the work of such free will to picture, for its own purposes, the world as an unfree, a causally connected, an existing system; and if it is the triumph of modern psychology to master even the best in man, the will, and to dissolve even the will into its atomistic sensations, and their causal unfree play, we are blind if we forget that this transformation and construction is itself the work of the will which dictates ends, and is the finest herald of its freedom."

Again he says: "Values and duties, freedom and responsibility belong to the inner life in its real activity, but not to the system of psychological facts into which we have transformed the inner experience."

The effort to put God out of His universe, to bind all down under a blind, mechanical fate, ever recurs under various mutations of philosophy. Yet a historical review of the race shows that man refuses to give up belief in a region where the will, be it human or divine, chooses... a region of freedom and responsibility. Neither man nor God can be reduced to a mere cog on a wheel.

Having, then, established the fact that there must be First Cause or causes outside of and overruliug the mechanical second causes, we come to the more specific problem, Is there a First Cause of Evil? Those who believe in God as monotheistically conceived, cannot think of Him as less than perfect. Hence they cannot attribute evil to God. But in this present realm of cause and effect, there is no place for an effect without a cause. Evil must have a source outside of God and outside of this law of cause and effect. This leads us to another free-will First Cause.

DEMONISM

The facts of demonism confirm this postulate. The evil quality manifested in demonism cannot be accounted for except on the hypothesis of Satanic origin. Question will be raised, Are there not cases of good spirits taking control of a dissociated personality? Such may be possible. Joan of Arc and Swedenborg at once come to mind. Yet they do not seem to have lost their personalities. The good spirits seemed to communicate with them and help them in their normal personalities. What looks more like control by good spirits is to be seen in some of the cases reported by the Societies for Psychic Research, e.g., the case of D D. Home (reported by Sir William Crookes) and that of William Stainton Moses (studied by Edmund Gurney and F. W. H. Myers).

If these cases are good spirits, then it strengthens my claim that the moral quality must have an origin. In any case they are not to be classified with demonism, except in so far as both are hysteria, for they do not appear in the environment which produces demonism. As they are sporadic, we must infer special causation with each case, whether physical or psychic. The demonized are a well-defined class of cases, readily diagnosed by those familiar with the malady. Those demonized, so far as reports go, are all marked by wickedness, malice, evil of every kind, with no good, no love, no kindliness. Neither I nor any of those who have observed these cases have ever heard of a good demon. Even the healing of diseases is done in a spirit of grasping for power over the sufferer, giving a temporary respite, but demanding perpetual slavery.

Take Miss King's night-walker, No. 113. She was an old woman with a little grandchild. For fourteen years she had walked the streets of Yaugchow every night. The policemen all knew her. She had no volition of her own. It would be benevolent indeed to heal a patient and subject her to such bondage! No one who knows demonism in its haunts would raise any question that it is absolutely and irrevocably evil. If we take these as auto-suggestion, then the environment must bear the blame; but environment which can produce a uniformly evil affection like this must be itself evil, and must have an evil origin. If the presence of evil in the world in a general way presupposes an evil First Cause, how much more when we see evil en bloc?

That there is a Satan and that Satan is responsible for demonism is put beyond question by the fact that the lines of demarcation betwTeen the countries which have not demonism and those which have It coincide with the limits of Christian influence. In the West, the only genuine case of demonism I have found, in present times, is that of Gottleibin Dittus, recorded in the 'Biography of Rev. Jno. Christopher Blumhardt.' This was a young woman, sickly, shy, very religious. She told Blumhardt that a woman or her acquaintance, who had died two years before, appeared to her. Every time she appeared the girl had a convulsion. After recovering consciousness, she had no recollection of events. There were unaccountable noises, windows rattled, plaster fell. When Blutnhardt invoked the name 'Jesus,' she shivered and a voice not her own replied; 'That name I cannot bear.' There was talking in the demon personality. The demons claimed to be 1,067 in number. They spoke all the languages of Europe and some that Blumhardt and others did not recognize. She was healed by fasting and prayer.

It has been supposed that the case known as 'Old Stump,' studied by Dr. Ira Barrows, was demonism. With this young girl, her right hand seems to form an independent personality which she calls Old Stump. She seems to know nothing of what Old Stump does. At times she raves, tears hair and clothing, but Old Stump tries to hold the left hand down. She dislikes Old Stump, although the latter is benevolent in disposition. She pounds and pricks this right hand. At night, when apparently asleep, she sits up and the right hand writes, but when she wakes she knows nothing of what she wrote. She writes poetry, Latin and French with Old Stump, although normally she knows neither Latin nor French. When her delirium is at its height, the right hand is rational, asking and answering questions in writing, trying to pull the bedclothes over her, etc.

Now this case resembles demonism in that it is a dissociation, but there the resemblance ends. It does not come from fear of demons, there is no demon control, no evil quality in Old Stump. When not in delirium, the normal personality does not reappear, thus showing more or less permanent,' diseased conditions. Jung's patient, a girl who in the dissociated personality took the name 'Ivenes,' also resembles demonism. She once took part in table turning for fun, and thus it was discovered that she was a medium. She would have periods of trance, ending usually in catalepsy.

Once she was hysterically blind for half an hour. In the trances, under the 'guidance' of her grandfather, whom she had never seen, she would see spirits, both benevolent and malevolent. When in the deep trance she would speak in an altered voice and in high classical German, such as her grandfather, a clergyman, would have used. She represented herself to have been previously incarnated a number of times, thus becoming the mother of thousands. A mystic system of world forces was developed by Ivenes, which she claimed was given her by the 'star-dwellers,' but after this the seances ceased. She could not revive them, and six months later was caught in deception. Jung diagnosed this case as arising from sexual disturbances of puberty. There was clear hereditan influence and marked maladjustment to environment. The mother was rough and vulgar, while the father was too busy to notice her. She would be afraid to go home. She was absent-minded, fond of day-dreaming. The matter did not originate in superstition, there

DEMONISM

was no demon, no evil quality, no antagonism to the name 'Jesus,' none of the most marked symptoms of demonism. In Western asylums are many insane and hysterics who manifest symptoms somewhat resembling demonism; but to identify them would be as scientific as to identify malaria and diphtheria because both have fever, or delirium tremens and typhoid because both have delirium.

While in enlightened Christian countries demonism is so rare as to be a negligible quantity, we have seen that it appears in multitudes wherever Christ is not known. China, Japan, Korea are full of it. India, too, is a non-Christian land, for the British Government zealously protects Buddhism and Mohammedanism. Nevius gives two capable witnesses to demonism there, the one a bishop and the other a British official. Miss MacNaughton sends me two clear cases from her India hospital. James Moore Hicksou, known as 'The Healer,' writes me that in India he healed two hundred cases of demonism in one meeting. In New Zealand, for twenty years, Rev. Canon Williams has been observing demonism and sends notes on six cases he has witnessed. This shows its prevalence in the Pacific Islands. Elsewhere I have given evidence for Africa and the Moslem lands. In all these countries the demonism is clearly differentiated from the insanities and dissociations seen in Christian lands. It originates in superstition; it is characteristically evil; there are always one or more demons in control; the affection passes from one person to another and back again; there is intense hatred of the name 'Jesus', they are healed by prayer and command in the name of Jesus.

This line of cleavage between Christian and other lands cannot be ignored. How can it be accounted for? By racial characteristics? In the past, from Egypt downwards the Western world has seen successive races reach high intellectual development. In the East, China and India have at times surpassed the West intellectually. Yet none of these races rid the world of demonism. Or can we account for this line of cleavage on the ground that Christianity is the product of higher education? But why is it that Europe and America have this education and other lands have it not? The only comprehensive differential is the Christian religion. It must therefore be causal rather than resultant.

Japan now ranks as one of the great powers. In medicine she has made such advances that the sanitation in her armies was the wonder of the world; and her scientists are inventors of the first rank. Yet Japan has not rid her country of demonism. Educational systems based on wrong conceptions of divinity have never been able to throw off demonism. It is safe to predict that Japan will continue to have demonism so long as she has idolatry, which is the worship of demons in the primary sense of the term.

The only system that has gotten rid of demonism is that based on what I have called normal, scientific religion, the monotheistic conception of systematized law under Supreme guidance. This system must be based on fact, on truth. And, furthermore, monotheism must be imbued with the Spirit of the Christ. This Spirit threw off the shackles of Judaism ; in the Reformers it threw off papal ecclesiasticism; in Copernicus, Galileo, Columbus, it threw off the autocracy of mistaken dogma; it is this living Spirit in man that is freeing the world from the degrading influence of the Anti-Divine, the Satan.

CHAPTER VIII

Satanic Dissociation

Since there is, then, an ultimate source of evil in the world, a Satan to whom or to which we may refer the environment in which demonism occurs, need we also infer a more direct Satanic influence in the actual cases of demonism?

Science has discovered truths which Aesculapius, e.g., could not have believed possible, namely, that maladies physically manifested, hysteria, asthma, and the like, may be traced back to psychic causes. There may be yet higher possibilities before us. It is clearly within the range of anticipation that men, on scientific grounds, independently of religious faith, may come to recognize both God and Satan. At any rate, science is now removing many of the obstacles to the recognition of spiritualities. The law of suggestion provides a tenable hypothesis on which to understand their influence over men.

We have seen that the influence of the Divine is ordinarily mediate, IE, by the disposing of conditions, the manipulating of secondary causes, working through and by this vast system which He has created. If there be Satanic influence, we may reasonably understand it in a similar way, that Satan has knowledge of, and power over, world conditions, not to arbitrarily interfere with, but to work through, natural law. This brings up the question, Does Satan have such power over human affairs as to cause dissociation, not only as the original source of evil in the environmental conditions, but by purposive psychic influence, over an individual, by volitional suggestion, whether with or without second causes as the case may be?

DEMONISM

The proposition that there is a Satan, who does influence men by suggestion is, of course, acceptable to those who acknowledge the tenets of the Christian churches. Indeed they may accept the proposition so readily as to confuse the condition of Satanic dissociation with the evil tendencies of minds not dissociated. A tyrant who, in his lust for power, slays innocent citizens is instigated by Satan, but he is not demon 'possessed.' There is no change of personality. For the cause of lust and cruelty- back of even 'social suggestibility'- no adequate interpretation has been found except on the hypothesis of a Satan with power to suggest. If there be, then, a Satan with power to influence men in the ordinary sense, will not such a Satan be able also to hypnotize by volitional suggestion? If so, the dissociating of the demonized may be, in all or some of the cases, due to such suggestion. Satan would then control the demonized personalities, directing them even as the human operator controls his hypnotized subject. In demonism there are data which tend to substantiate this tentative hypothesis as a matter of fact.

In Western lands automatic, 'accidental' dissociation more usually occurs where there are pathological or psycho-pathological predisposing factors. Looking over thirty-one well-known cases, I find only four in which there is not clear record of trauma, epilepsy, lesion, exhaustion, or at least continued hysteric and neurasthenic conditions. Even of the four some authorities question the data in the Mary Reynolds case and attribute the Ansel Bourne case to epilepsy in youth. But volitional suggestion is not in any way dependent on such predisposing factors. Forel says: "I cannot emphasize too strongly that suggestibility is an absolutely normal characteristic of the normal human brain."

The Dictionary of Philosophy and Psychology takes this as the consensus of scientific opinion. This is not incompatible with Sidis's position that hypnosis is abnormal as contrasted with normal suggestibility. Hypnotization by normal suggestion brings about the abnormal condition, hypnosis. Now in demonism the most hearty, robust, stolid are affected. My No. 58 I found to be a buxom young woman with a baby and pregnant. Her mother, fifty nine years old, walked in five miles to see her. The old lady was the picture of health. She reported her husband also healthy, and that her seven children were hearty, even this one having never had any illness until the demon came on her. No. 58 was given a clinical examination by J. W. Hewett, M.R.C.S., L.R.C.P., and pronounced normal.

My No. 405 is a little old lady of sixty-four as spry as a kitten. If there be pathological conditions, it would take a clinical sleuth to detect them. Yet she has been liable to demonism practically all her life. When I last saw her, October 12th, 1920, she had two typical spells. They would come on with terrific yawns. The face assumed an aspect of malignity with a defiant pertness pathetically inconsistent in such a wizened little old body. When led out to be photographed, the demon struggled and fought. During the hymn she lay prone on the ground, chanting in a weird monotone. But immediately afterwards, while praying, I peeped up and almost laughed to see her standing beside me normal, silently looking on with a curious, interested attention. Unfortunately, as she is stone deaf, we cannot reach her mind, to cure her. In many of the cases there is no indication of pathological or psycho-pathological conditions other than the environment.

Now is such hypnotization adequately accounted for on the hypothesis of autosuggestion? To say that the environmental conditions are psycho-pathological does not cover the ground. Environmental conditions may give the soil for psychogenesis, but that does not give a neurological predisposition or a nervous instability in the individual. With this class of cases, so many of whom are otherwise in normal health, the dissociating is artificial rather than spontaneous, and presupposes suggestion from without. The characteristic evil quality points to Satan as the hypnotizer.

The thought content of the demonized and the psychic attitudes cannot be accounted for subjectively. The fact that the demons know all about the primary consciousness, would indicate previous co-conscious existence, and thus would account for some of the apparent occultism. But even this cannot account for the knowledge of, the fear and hatred of Jesus. This is a characteristic of demonism and is manifested in some cases, which neither consciously nor subconsciously have ever received such information from human kind.

In Dr. Wood's case, No. 101, at the mention of Jesus, the demonized patient immediately showed a change and in five minutes was normal. No. 109, on hearing the name, would curse Miss King. Mrs. Paxton's case, No. 118, manifested hatred of the name. No. 4, when demonized, used to curse Mr. Meng, but after the latter became a Christian, the demon dared not do so, and would shun him. No. 58 could say anything except the name 'Jesus.' In teaching her to pray, we would lead her up to the words just before it, and then she would balk. She told me that 'it' did not allow her to say it. In No. 143, Rev. W. H. Hudson, D.D., was walking along the streets of a small town, where no missionary lived. A demonized man, who had never seen him before, called out in the dialect he used, "Servant of God, what have you come here for?" In the conversation following, Dr. Hudson gave the man a prayer, and he was healed, but later he was taken back into idolatrous environment.

The hostile influences prevailed, and he died. Two of the cases reported by Rev. Jonathan Goforth, D. B., manifested strong hatred of Jesus. One of them No. 160, was wild, gesticulating. The eyes looked unnatural, and rolled around. A missionary was praying and used the name, 'Jesus of Nazareth.' Instantly the patient had a paroxysm of hatred, which was repeated every time the name was mentioned. With the other, No. 159, a Lutheran missionary lady was entering a certain town. A woman, whom she supposed to be crazy, stopped her chair, crying out, 'We do not want your Jesus doings here.' She followed after the chair, making demonstrations until they reached the mission. There it was recognized as demonism and healed. The German case to which I have referred showed this same hostility.

Miss MacNaughton, of India, sends the following interesting case. One day a strange woman came to the hospital. Every now and then from within her would come the sound as of a cock crowing. Then she would become wild. Miss MacNaughton said to the Indian lady doctor, "We must kneel down and pray in the name of Jesus." At that a different voice from within the woman spoke, saying, "No, that name I cannot take," and she was thrown down, apparently with great force to the ground. At the mention of the name 'Jesus,' the spirit would seem to be in a frenzy, and then suddenly she began to sing to a beautiful tune a most wonderful poem, evidently made up at the time, for one verse was about the hospital, but the demon said that the Name it could not and never would take ; that it would take the name of Mohammed and the names of the Hindu deities, but not that other name.

I grant that there are two methods of interpreting this hatred and fear of the name of Jesus. The one is, that the secondary personality recognizes the name Jesus as a concept hostile to itself, merely a concept with no foundation in fact, and this automatically excites the hostility. The other interpretation is that the secondary personality is of an objective origin, that a morally evil power has by utilizing the law of suggestion brought

DEMONISM

about the decomposition of the personality, or maybe has taken advantage of a case of auto-suggestion, but in some way has gotten control of the subconscious self. The fear and hatred of Jesus on the part of the second personality, thus set off, comes from a morally evil hypnotizer, Satan, with whom it is en rapport. That the second is the true interpretation I maintain on the following ground:

I. The regularity with which this symptom appears.

II. The history of hysteria and hypnotism does not suddenly conceive such a fear of the book unless she had been informed and influenced by a mentality that did know these things, the same mentality which implants this fear on all under its control, whether in China, in Korea, in India, or in Germany?

III. Nor can we find in the environment anything to account for the uniform hatred and fear of Jesus.

The Chinese at large do not believe in Him. My No. 79 had been afflicted for ten years, the trouble beginning before her marriage. Later the husband, No. 80, and one of the children, No. 81, were liable to the influence. A relative, Wang Tao Ru, told them Jesus could heal the trouble. But a neighbor, Li Ta Hsiu, said he could heal it. Living a few miles away, he proposed to hang up scrolls, worship the demon, and thus attract his majesty to take up his abode with Li This meant sacrifice, but for it he was paid twenty thousand cash, a sum sufficient to support a poor family for months. Li's proposition was accepted even though it cost all this money. Yet, strange to say, it fails. Only brief relief is noticeable. Later, others renew Wang's suggestion, and the family decide to try Christianity. After the first failure, they would, of course, be less receptive. Yet the power of Jesus is manifested. On March 16, 1917, No. 80 came to church well, and afterward his wife also was healed. This could not have been accomplished by another fictitious suggestion, for there was nothing in the environment to make the latter suggestion more effective than the former one. Oh, but some one will say, this is easily explained. The conscious mind accepted Li's suggestion and the subconscious Wang's, thus inhibiting the former and making the latter effective. But why should the subconscious mind accept it? Remember that the subconscious has a wonderful faculty of detecting frauds. Had the name 'Jesus' also been based on falsehood, we cannot doubt that it would have been detected.

Again, supposing that auto-hypnotization could, on a purely subjective basis, account for the disintegrating and the reintegrating, the cases reported of demons transferred from one person to another cannot be adequately accounted for without assuming an objective agency. Take my cases Nos. 3 and 25, a young wife and her husband. The young man's father had been both wizard and robber. He would have spells of demonism, chanting, etc. While he lived they were not affected. After his death, the daughter-in-law alone was affected. The symptoms were so identical with those of the old wizard that the community considered it his spirit troubling her.

She was healed in the home of her Christian brother. Then the affection took her husband. That this was not merely subjective auto-hypnotization is shown by the fact that of the three none were affected synchronously and by the coincidence of the dates. What prevented auto-hypnotization with the young couple all the time they lived with the old man? Must we postulate, on a purely accidental basis, positive suggestion for him and negative suggestion for them? And shall we also postulate an accidental withdrawing of the negative suggestion on the death of the father and on the healing of the wife? So far as we can see, had the father not died, the wife would not have been taken. Had she not beer, healed, her husband would not have been taken.

Rev. Canon Williams gives a clear case of transference. A mother had been afflicted for some years, occasionally having periods when she would be under strong control for days at a time. She would not speak nor take notice of any one, and had a fixed stare. At the end of 1918, her eldest daughter suddenly developed the same symptoms. Immediately the mother became well and continued so for nine months during the whole period that the daughter was afflicted. The daughter was taken to an asylum and spent eight months there under strong control all the time. Then she suddenly recovered and the mother was again taken.

No. 75 presents further considerations. A man was afflicted. The house caught fire. No. 75, then normal, brought him out and laid him in a furrow. From that time the patient was healed, but No. 75 was afflicted and was so when our people saw him. Note that in this case there was no anticipatory suggestion from family history or otherwise. Nor was there any apparent cause for the healing. We might suppose that the shock of the fire healed the one and subjective auto-hypnotization caused the affliction of the other. But how account for the remarkable coincidence?

No. 124 was reported by Mrs. Anna Sykes, Rev. Tracy I. Moffett and Dr. Geo. C. Worth. They all knew the parties, the patient herself having lived with them for ten years after the occurrences. I asked Mr. Moffett and Dr. Worth whether either of them had any doubts about the facts. Both replied, "None at all." Dr. Worth, who stands high in his profession, continued: "The case is one well attested in every way and there can be no doubt about it. They were all sensible people, not neurotic, not the kind you would expect to have such an experience." This patient became afflicted. She would have spells in which she would be rigid for several days. The Christians, when summoned, first required them to put away all idolatry. There was, behind the house, a grove and shrine peculiarly sacred. Even these were removed. The patient was healed, but a relapse occurred when the husband brought back the idols. The Christians came again. They prayed. Some of them were stroking the patient's legs. She said: "Now he has my throat- now he has gone to my feet." The old preacher, making a dash at the demon, said, "I'll get him."

She continued, "Now he is over there in the corner- there he goes out of the window." As she said this, a young man looking in the window, cried out, "He has come into me!" and fell down. The preacher told the family that if they would bring him to them, they could cure him, but if they took him to the priests, he would die. They went to the priests, and he did die a few days afterwards with no apparent cause.

Here again we have a clear-cut case of transference and this death from suggestion recalls Boerhaave's well known experiment. He got a condemned criminal and told him he was going to kill him at a set time. When the time came, he bandaged the criminals eyes, arranged warm water to drip, giving the suggestion of bleeding, and pretended to open a vein. Death resulted. Now note, in this case a directing mind, with strong psychic influence, prepares the subject by anticipatory suggestion and devices of every kind, leading him up to the culminating suggestion. If I could prove that a boy, with no directing mind, and no anticipatory preparation, had died from a sudden notion that a demon was flying in his direction, I should have outdone Boerhaave. It is a simpler hypothesis that in this case also there was a directing mind, which was preparing the subject, and which gave the fatal suggestion.

There are cases in which the demonism could not have been caused by subjective auto-hypnotization. In these studies I have not drawn from the Scriptures, lest I seem to be influenced by religious prejudices. Yet the facts in the New Testament are at least as well attested as those of profane history. In these records the case of the demoniac and the swine is reported by Matthew, Mark and Luke, historians no less reliable than Thucydides and Livy. Their history is accepted as authentic by a large part of the human race. Even those who oppose the religious tenets of Christianity have no charges to bring against the personal character of these historians. While there are men who doubt some of their statements as being scientifically impossible, yet their records have never been disproved in any particular, and as to this case they were in all probability among the band of eyewitnesses to the incident.

The scientific objection to this case is now much lessened. The probability is that animals may be hypnotized. True, the passive immobility seen in Kircher's famous experiments with the hen and chalk line, in the charming of birds by serpents, etc., has been classified as cataplexy, as distinguished from catalepsy so common with hypnotism. But Myers held that animals are probably hypnotizable. Thompson J. Hudson in his popular book, 'The Law of Psychic Phenomena' thinks the methods of animal trainers are based on this principle. They are not unlike Braid's methods of hypnotizing by mechanical processes. Ernst Mangold wrote a book on 'Hypnotism and Catalepsy of Animals xompared with human Hypnosis.' This gives us a tenable hypothesis as to the principles underlying the swine case. But it could not have been hypnotization by auto-suggestion. Nor can we consider it hypnotism by Jesus. As speech was impossible, he would have had to use the mechanical methods.

Judging from the records and the circumstances he did not use them. We may then take this as a historical record of a case of demonism in which there must have been objective

DEMONISM

hypnotizing agency. As confirmatory consider my No. 151. Rev. and Mrs. H. J. Mason, English missionaries with years of experience in China, have come in contact with something like a thousand cases. Mrs. Mason reports a case in which a whole family were demonized. On one occasion, the family dog was similarly affected and bit the patient. Mrs. Mason visited the family shortly afterwards, and the circumstances were such that she was convinced that the dog also was demonized. We have no opportunity for closer investigation, but with the New Testament record before us and considering the witness's reliability, experience and intimate knowledge, we cannot lightly disregard her testimony.

As bearing on the question of demonism without auto-suggestion, we must consider the demonized infants. I have a number of such cases. The Chinese differentiate demonism from other diseases, and my experience is that the diagnosis of the native doctors in cases of demonism is remarkably correct. Rev. Canon Williams also reports an infant of two and a half years, which he believes to be demonized. Mark 9:21 seems to be a case in point. With these infants, even though speech is wanting, yet there are strong indications of psychogenic demonism.

Take No. 410. It occurred in a demonized family, and the symptoms, with the chameleon ways of hysteria, were identical with those of the other cases. There was clear psychogenic history. The family had been Taoist worshipers, animists, vegetarians, fearing demons and witches. Two sisters-in-law, no blood kin, and a daughter become dissociated. Spells occur with characteristic irregularity, in which they talk as demons. The physical symptoms are vomiting, purging, and insomnia, symptoms which suddenly cease with Nos. 345 and 347, when healed psychically. No. 345 has a baby. Within three days it has spells just like those of the adults. The spells come and go at any time, and continue a year or more with no general effect on the patient's health. At first there is purging as with the others. Later it is a matter of general discomfort and fretfulness. After a year some fever occurs with the spells but no chill. Once a rash comes out, stays a day or so and disappears. Between spells the child is well. In its own home it is more inclined to the spells, and when away, especially in the chapel it looks jolly and well- takes the baptismal service as a joke gotten up for its amusement. In the home I felt like giving the baby a dose, but in the chapel I felt like saying: "That child is no more ill than I am." Such indications point to hysteria. What shall we make of this case? When the mother was dissociated, were the physical changes- for hysteria has a physical side to it- such as to be transmitted to the infant? We know that permanent constitutional characteristics are transmitted by heredity. A parent's tastes, habits, traits of character reappear in the children or descendants. But that functional psychopathic conditions are so transmitted is a more difficult proposition.

Sidis denies that they are hereditary. In this case the physical change in the brain and nervous system of the parent were such as to be relieved by faith in Jesus. Can it be that she could transmit to her infant qualities not permanent to herself?

Some nervous instability may have been transmitted, though even that is unlikely. The baby was a boy and thus less liable to hysteria. I saw the mother a number of times. Indeed I slept in the mud hut with eight people including Nos. 345, 347, 410, and the father. The adults are sunburned, work-hardened people. When her husband started to the stream to bring a cask of water, weighing a hundred and fifty pounds or more, No. 345 remarked that she feared he could not carry it alone, voluntarily went, and shouldered half the load. Such a woman would hardly transmit neurasthenia or hysterical temperament to her child!

Nos. 323, 324, 325, 411 and an infant, not numbered,

give an interesting series. A grandmother in old age is suddenly seized with hysterical pains and then convulsions. She is clearly demonized, chanting and singing and demanding worship. She dies under it. A few days later a two months' old grandchild, well and hearty at night, in the morning is found, outside the bed cover, dead, with blood from nose and eyes. Four days later the childs mother (No. 325) and a sister in law (No. 324) are taken with clearly marked demonism. The demon speaking through them claims to have killed the grandmother and the baby. They are healed by Christianity.

But No. 325 has another baby (No. 411). It is soon taken with what the family and friends recognize as the same trouble. It too is healed by Christian methods. Now this might be a case of epilepsy by physical heredity. But to support such a hypothesis we must suppose the demonism transmitted to the daughters in law by psychic suggestion- they are no blood kin- and then, skipping a generation, reappearing in one or both infants by heredity. And the old lady's case answers more readily to a psychogenic than to an organic diagnosis.

There was no report of epileptic symptoms until she was about sixty years old. She lived in a neighborhood where demons abounded. Our old friends, No. 58 and No. 72, with their numerous families of demons were near by. Everybody believed in and dreaded mythical Foxes and Weasels- with a capital letter! Her physical symptoms were just such as would occur with subconscious system organized on these weasel concepts. And again, other members of her family were not affected so long as she lived. As soon as she is dead the baby dies mysteriously, possibly killed by the mother though the indications are against that theory, or possibly dying from psycho-neurotic conditions induced by the demonism, e.g., epileptiform convulsions. Then the two young women are taken with the same symptoms. Later, the second baby is afflicted in the same way. The symptoms, the circumstances, the transferences point strongly to psychogenic demonism rather than epilepsy. But if so, to account for the transferences to infants unable to talk we must infer an objective influence for there could be no subjective auto-suggestion. As the affections belong to the characteristically evil species of dissociation, this objective influence would be Satan.

Satanic psychic influence such as would account for these cases- swine, dog, babies- does not, of course, antagonize scientific principles. There could be no demonism without the environment. But the environment could not reach them in the ordinary way by mental concepts, fear of demons. We must infer a source of suggestion, a Satan.

We may now make certain general inductions:

I. Independently of the question of revelation, facts indicate that there must be a Satan, an original source of evil in the world, and the ultimate source of what we may now call Satanic Dissociation.

II. The hypothesis that this Satan may influence human beings by volitional suggestion, and control dissociated personalities, does not contradict science.

III. This hypothesis is borne out by the facts of demonism.

CHAPTER IX

Demons and Spirits of the Dead

Since, then, there is a Satan, the original source of demonism, and since the dissociated personalities of the demonized are under the control of Satan, operating by the law of suggestion, how does Satan exercise this control, directly or through emissaries? Is it Satan or a Satanic demon which controls the demonized?

On this particular point it is necessary to consider the teachings of the Scriptures. Not to seek proof of my position; for the object of this book is to prove the Scriptures by the facts, not to prove the facts by the Scriptures. But those of us whose life-time views have been formed on the Scripture basis, must first clear our path, before we can get an unobstructed view of this problem. The Bible teaches that there is a Satan, and that there are Satanic demons. But does the Bible teach that demons or the spirits of the dead can communicate with the living? On this point it is not so fully committed as we may have thought. This problem depends largely on the mode of communication between Satan and men.

The Bible constantly speaks of Satan tempting men, with no hint of intermediate agencies and in language that seems to imply direct communication. Satan 'tempted' Jesus, 'entered into' Judas, 'as a roaring lion, walketh about, seeking whom he may devour.' He 'plants the tares', 'snatches away the seed,' 'blinds the minds of the unbelieving.' We are told, 'Do not give place to the Devil,' 'resist the Devil,' 'stand against the wiles of the Devil.' John writes to the young men because they have overcome the evil one; we pray to be kept from the evil one; the Lord guards us from the evil one. The wicked are said to be of their father the

DEMONISM

Devil. Cain was of the evil one. Paul wrote of the law of sin working in our members, of our fulfilling the desires of the flesh and of the mind. The tenor of the Scriptures seems to be that Satan is a spirit, limited neither by time nor by space, who has implanted an evil nature in man, and who can communicate directly with men, having no need of intermediaries. The passages which teach that demons communicate with men might, with cause sufficient, be treated as anthropomorphic or merely figurative.

Those, therefore, who think this to be the true interpretation can leave the demons out of the case and consider the demonized as dissociated personalities controlled by Satan, just as we have been accustomed to think of a murderer being influenced by him.

On the other hand, at least two passages do teach that demons tempt men in normal life. In Eph. 6:12 we are said to wrestle "against the principalities, against the powers, against the world rulers of this darkness, against spiritual wickedness in high places." Again in Rev. 16: 14 we read of 'spirits of demons,' working signs, going forth to draw the kings of the earth to battle against God. With regard to the Bible teachings on this subject, the International Standard Bible Encyclopedia (Orr) notes that the Old Testament never speaks of the demonized- God taught the Jews to hate idolatry and all connected with it- and that the New Testament does not discuss the demons. Jesus unquestionably refers them to Satan, but he had nothing to say about the rabbinical discussions as to whether they were spirits of the dead, fallen angels, or what. He does in some cases speak of the demon as being an entity other than the patient and not Satan. In Lu. 10:20 he says, 'In this rejoice not, that the spirits are subject unto you.' In Mt. 12:43 and Lu. 11:24 he speaks of the demon, cast out, going through 'waterless places,' seeking rest, and bringing back seven other spirits into the patient. In Lu.

DEMONISM

8:31 the demon showed fear of 'the abyss,' and that whole narrative seems to put Jesus' imprimatur on the conception of the demon as an individual entity.

To take the view that Satanic suggestion, with the demonized and perhaps with the normal, comes through subsidiary spirits, gives a more literal interpretation of the Scriptures and confirms the thought of saints and poets, who themselves rose above crude superstitions. The distinction between these two conceptions may be illustrated thus. Direct communication, with no intermediaries, the theory which I have suggested as possible, would be like a vast telephonic system, wireless if you please, Satan himself communicating with, influencing, giving suggestions to men and in this way causing demonism. The second theory would make communication between Satan and men more like that, for instance, between the President and the people of the United States. It is not necessary for everybody to see him or speak to him. One may write a letter, drop it in the box. It reaches the President's office and is answered according to his wishes, yet he may not see it. On this theory, both God and Satan are the centers of vast systems of personalities, radiating everywhere, systems in which subsidiaries do the will of their executives.

The study of demonism gives ground for believing that this latter is the correct view.

Aside from Scripture we know enough about Satan to justify the belief that HE must have personality- and the same could be said of God. The distinction between a Satan conceived of as an impersonal force or principle and a personal Devil, is, to some extent, that between the simple and the complex, the systematized. In the human organism disorganized sensations, reactions, ideas, memories are not personalities, but when coordinated into a system exercising the higher functions of purpose, thought, reason, then they become a personality, able to frame the 'ego,' to say 'I.' So in the spiritual world, an organism, in which forces and principles operate, and which, on the other hand, can manipulate scientific principles to its own ends, must be a personality, Forces and principles do not have personality. When one presses the button, he does not have to ask the electricity whether he may turn on the light. When one falls out of a tree, gravitation does not consider whether he is to fall or fly. The life principle cannot decide whether one is to live or die. Forces and principles are mechanical, dead. What we must infer as to Satan- that he is one who resists God, who puts the evil nature in man, who tempts man, who can manipulate natural law- would be impossible except in a personality. It implies mental powers and the manipulating of scientific principles rather than dead mechanism.

Recognizing this fact, it would be banal to believe in a single evil personality. Shall we postulate myriads of human, but only two non-human personalities, God and Satan? Personality on the part of Satan implies the existence of subsidiary, evil personalities, i.e., Satanic demons, even though there were no Scripture on the subject. Satan would be lonely indeed if he had no company. Since, then, there are demons, and since we saw in Chaps. VII and VIII that demonism is from Satan, the inference would be that demons are the medium of communication.

A second argument may be based on the personal qualities of the demons, especially as manifested in cases of transference. Do not mistake me. I am not arguing that the qualities of personality manifested in demonism prove demonic origin. If I did so, some would at once fling Sally and Twoey and Leonie and Ivenes at me. They had personality but were not demons. The proofs of Satanic control in demonism have already been given in previous chapters. The question now is as to distinctions of personality, not in the demonized humans, but in the hypnotizing agent, Satan. The influences, the controls which dominate the demonized have differing dispositions, faculties, desires; they come and they go ; recognized in A, they reappear in B and C.

We saw in Chap. VIII that cases of transference necessarily imply an objective agency. Mere auto-suggestion might account for a 'new' demon taking its traits from an 'old' one, but could not account for the demon leaving the original case, nor for the remarkable coincidences manifested. Now, what is it that is transferred? We have seen that a demon is the evil part of a man's nature dissociated by and under the power of Satan. Is it this dissociated personality which is transferred? We must reject this for two reasons.

I. When the transference takes place, the patient is reintegrated, the first and second personalities reuniting. There is now no dissociated personality to 'migrate.'

II. To maintain that a Sally or a Twoey, e.g., could enter the personalities of others than Miss Beauchamp and Alma Z., would mean that living beings could become demons- a proposition I, for one, should not like to undertake.

It is not a transference of the dissociated personality, but of the hypnotizing agent. Now we have seen that Satan is the hypnotizer in demonism. What is transferred must, then, be either the one great Satan personality, or a representative of him- an emanation, capable of exercising his powers. But the controls, all exhibiting the Satanic hatred and fear of Jesus, each have their own desires, purposes, thoughts, and are readily distinguished from one another. To see this, I will narrate a few cases. No. 153 I clip from The Watchman Magazine. This was a woman in Korea, thirty-five years of age. A year previous to this occurrence she had been taken with a fear, and began to wander about the hills. When she would lie down, the whole body would writhe. She went to the Christians. When they worshiped, she made all manner of noises. An open Bible was placed on her head from behind. She snatched it away, saying she was afraid of it. Then a hymn book was placed there, but she laughed, saying it could not hurt head. All this was in spite of the fact that she could not read.

When the Christians prayed, the demon asked, "Where will you send us?"- for it claimed to be five in number. The leader said it might go wherever it pleased. Then the demon begged to be allowed to enter another person. The Christians refused and prayed harder. At last the demon said that in three days it would leave the woman and go to a certain creek. On the third day she was taken with violent crying and wallowed on the ground. When she ceased to cry, she was normal, and ever since has been a happy Christian.

No. 149, from New Zealand, I have related in Chapter I. After eight or nine demons had been exorcised by the last and strongest control, which spoke English though the patient knew only Maori, refused to come out. When finally yielding, this spirit begged to be allowed to enter an afflicted child there present, and on being refused threatened to injure the body of the patient, mentioning four possible ways of doing so. Finding no recourse, the spirit threw her off the seat into the middle of the room, where she was suspended by levitation at an angle of forty-five degrees for quite half a minute and then fell in collapse. Thereafter she was entirely free. Miss A. Mildred Cable, in her 'The Fulfillment of a Dream,' gives this incident.

A demon driven from a man who had become a Christian, went to a village eight miles distant and took control of a young woman. Speaking through her, it forbade her marriage and manifested itself in the same manner as it had done in the man from whom it came, compelling her to rub one side of her face and head until there was no hair left. When questioned as to whence it came, the demon replied by giving the name of this man.

To the query 'why have you left him?' the reply was 'I have been turned out, for that man has become a Christian.' Compare also another of her cases. A daughter was married off, and was ill-treated in the husband's home. Finally she was poisoned. Of course none of her own family were present. A few days later, one of them, a strong young first cousin, while working in the fields, was seized with trembling and weeping. He said, "I am Lotus Bud: I was cruelly done to death. Why is there no redress?" The family gave reasons for their course, promising to do what the spirit wished. In an hour the spell passed off.

In all these cases the demon has the marks of an organized personality, distinguishable from Satan and from other demons.

A third argument I would base on the fact that demons either cannot, or at least ordinarily do not control two persons at the same time. This cannot be said of the Satan personality, who operates in all the world simultaneously. While I would not deny that there may be cases of the same spirit controlling two persons at once, yet I have never seen one. The universal testimony, so far as I know, of Chinese and Western observers, is that they do not. Even when report comes that a whole family is controlled by a spirit, I find on inquiry that it alternates from one to another. As No. 358 remarked in describing his case, ' when one of the family gets well, another is taken.' No. 459, with no leading questions on my part, said that when he would recover from a spell, it would take his wife, and when she recovered, it would go to one of the children. This point comes out clearly in a case reported by a lady who is now Mrs. W. E. Comerford. This No. 174 occurred eight or nine years ago in a village sixty It from Pingtu, Shantung Province, China. While this lady was conducting a meeting, an old woman came up, looked intently at her, and challenged the statement that there is a Devil, demanding that the missionary retract it. Seeing her threatening attitude, other women seized her, and then she broke into raving, tearing clothes, and scratching herself till she bled. Mrs. Comerford, at the instance of others, prayed for her, but saw no results. Later she recovered.

During this first rencontre there was present a young woman who was in the missionary's Bible class. She dashed under the benches, and afterwards said that from a child she had been afraid of this old woman, although she lived in the other end of the town. Shortly after the old woman's recovery, the young one was taken. The evangelist and others went and held worship with her. She was lying on the brick bed, raving and tearing herself like the old one did. The demon said, 'Put them all out.' She, in a different voice, would reply, 'No, you go.' Presently she had a convulsion. When it passed, she lay with a fixed stare, and presently fell asleep. After about three hours she waked normal. But now the old woman, in another part of the village, not knowing what had occurred, was herself again suddenly seized. Mrs. Comerford saw her, both after the first healing and during this second period. It was now autumn, and the missionaries wished to baptize the young woman. But circumstances prevented. In the spring a class was arranged for at a town eight li away. A Bible-woman went for this young woman and other inquirers. On the way she began to show fear. Time and again the Christians urged her to go on. At last she turned and ran home, raving and tearing herself. As soon as this occurred, the old woman again recovered, and so far as reports go, they remain in these respective conditions to the present time. If a missionary or Bible-woman goes near the young woman, she runs in and shuts the door, but the old woman is normal. The passages of the demon back and forth are clearly marked and it is evident that the two cannot be under control at the same time.

Seeing, then, that there must be personality, both for Satan and for demons ; that the controls which are transferred cannot be dissociated personalities, and are clearly distinguished from Satan and from one another; and that the demons do not control two persons at once; we would conclude that Satan's control of the demonized is through the medium of subsidiaries.

If, then, Satan works through subsidiary demons, can it be that he utilizes the spirits of the dead in this way? Was 'Lotus Bud' the girl herself or a spirit impersonating her?

Bible students have long puzzled over Samuel's return and the revelation of Moses and Elijah on the Mount of Transfiguration. The Societies for Psychic Research hold that personalities persist after death and can communicate with men. They have a mass of data, much of which has not been refuted. For example, J. H. Hyslop, for many years the leading spirit of the American Society for Psychic Research, told me before his death that he, a professor in Columbia University, and an unbeliever in spiritual matters, was convinced on this subject by the following case. One Frederick L,. Thompson, a goldsmith and engraver, with only crude ideas of painting, suddenly felt compelled to drop his work and go to painting. He had formerly had a mere speaking acquaintance with Swain Gifford. Now he felt that he himself was Gifford. He did not know until later that the latter had died six months before. His paintings showed art, and sold. One purchaser, James B. Townsend, not knowing his story, remarked that his work looked like Gifford's. Thompson became conscious of scenes and pictures which later proved to have been favorites of the painter. One scene of certain gnarled oaks which continually beset him, on being worked out, proved to have been known and painted by Gifford, and through mediums the location was discovered on a far-away spot never seen by Thompson. Having let Hyslop lock up some of his sketches, Thompson visited Gifford's studio, for the first time. It was just as the painter had left it and Thompson's breath was almost taken away to find on an easel an unfinished sketch exactly identical with one of those Hyslop had locked up.

In view of such cases, it is difficult to deny absolutely the possibility of communication, under some circumstances, between the dead and the living, and we shall watch with interest the investigations of these societies. But it is a safer proposition that for the spirits of the dead to communicate with the living, if possible, is a violation of natural law and of the conditions of their existence. We saw in Chapter III that the demon which speaks is really the dissociated part of the man himself, the 'old man,' the 'flesh.' Whatever the demons be that influence these dissociated personalities, giving color to their thoughts and acts, they cannot be the foxes and weasels and pigs that the demons often represent themselves to be.

By the same token we must discredit those which claim to be spirits of the dead. These chameleon ways indicate unreality. Again, that there are principles applying which prevent intercourse between the dead and the living is evidenced by the fact that ordinarily they do not communicate, and that what formerly was believed to be communication is now generally recognized as mere superstition. Race psychology has had such a recoil from the old view that spirits of the dead live all about us and catch us when they can, that the whole subject is in disrepute.

As things now stand, a modern mind, coming in contact with a personality dissociated on morally evil lines, finds it easier to believe, not that a grandfather's ghost has got the man, but that Satan controls the personality by suggestion, whether directly or through a subsidiary demon. But even Satan is not able to "possess" men ad libitum. All is under law, under scientific principles.

And nature's law says that men cannot be demonized except in places and under environment where men worship and fear demons.

CHAPTER X

Treatment of Demonism

Now that we know what demonism is, how is it to be cured, by science or by miracles? I say unquestionably that both principles are involved.

Misunderstanding of the term miracle is responsible for much of the conflict between science and religion. The crude conception of a miracle would demand that the healing be not only directly by God, but 'immediate,' excluding all means to an end. This view is justified neither by reason nor by Scripture. The most direct healing may yet be based on scientific principles. Edersheim had this in mind, when he wrote: "The objection to miracles, as such, proceeds on that false Supranaturalism, which traces a Miracle to the immediate fiat of the Almighty without any intervening links; and as already shown, it involves a vicious petitio principii."

A miracle is not necessarily, if ever, in violation of scientific principles. Science is knowledge of the laws of God, for there can be no law that is not of God. He does not deny Himself. God can make water go up a hill, but He would not make the law of gravitation take it up. That would indeed be a violation of one of His principles. He may suspend His laws, or use laws of which we are ignorant. We are learning more and more of the laws of God. Who would have thought a few years since that the human mind could cause paralysis, levitation, blindness, without the use of physical means? Some writers even claim that the human libido has creative powers. God, who made all these laws, knows and controls them as man never can. The day may come when we can prove demonstrably that mind, the Divine mind, can create.

DEMONISM

From this point of view we may define a miracle thus: "A Miracle is an Over-ruling of the Works of God in the Ordinary Course of Nature in Order to an Extraordinary, a Supernatural Manifestation of the Divine Volition in Response to an Appeal or a Definite Need."

With this view in mind, we can readily accept the scientific view that the flood was caused by a sudden elevation of the ocean bed, due to pressure of the ice-cap that covered Europe and America. That God was behind the matter was evidenced by Noah's history. As to the crossing of the Red Sea, we are told that it was a 'strong east wind' which, possibly at the ebb tide, swept a passage across the silted up mouth of the channel, leaving the waters on either side as a wall to the enemy-water does not have to stand up seven feet high to be a wall. But we must, with the Bible, hold that God sent that wind. And Moses would not have been such a fool as to bring that host into a culde sac. He was guided by the Divine Strategist. God timed the flight, timed the pursuit, timed the wind, and when the moment came, told Moses to sound the advance and smite the water.

God does not disdain to use means, even so unique as the ravens to feed Elijah. The miracles not yet understood- Jonah's experience, the virgin birth, the resurrection, the ascension- self-sufficient science complacently rejects, self-sufficient religion complacently accepts. The dynamic spirit of the truth does not refuse to believe what it cannot understand, but merely asks: Is there reliable testimony? Are the events such as would imply purposive Divine influence? and then works toward a comprehension of the methods of the Divine.

I maintain- and challenge contradiction- that to conceive of Jesus Christ as comprehending and controlling what we call science so thoroughly as to be able, not only to use its principles for the healing of the demonized, but also to establish a system which would in the hands of unscientific men overcome the power of Satan and rid the world of demonism, is an incalculably higher conception of the miracle idea than to hold merely that he had a fiat authority to order a demon out. This shows, independently of revelation, that the knowledge and power of Jesus were supernatural.

Holding in mind this view of the miracle, let us now study the treatment of demonism. We have found that the demon is the patient's wicked self, dissociated by the power of Satan and under his control. How shall we set about healing a case of demonism? The first thought is to tell the patient that it is not a demon that has control of him. But how far would you get on this line? The patient, even in the normal periods, would not be able to comprehend nor believe what you say. He knows that it is a demon, or thinks he does. The Dictionary of Psychological Medicine notes in connection with the Morzinnes epidemic that "nothing caused an attack so surely as the assertion that the convulsionnaires were not possessed."

Indeed, it is a demon; maybe not in the cuckoo-parasite sense, as formed and conceived; certainly not the weasel or fox demon, as the patient thinks; but a secondary personality controlled by Satan or by a Satanic spirit is a demon. It is not the patient himself. Investigators treat secondary personalities as real. They find it worse than useless to try to talk to one personality when another has control. Prince found himself puzzled and hindered when he thought he was talking to 'The Saint,' until he found that it was a personality he had not recognized, the one who later came to be known as 'The Realist.' Scientists adopt names for these personalities, addressing them as Sally, Leonie, Margaret. Frequently the personalities choose their own names or express a preference. The scientific study of dissociation is still in a formative state. In the cases studied, many of them arising out of pathological or psycho-pathological conditions, analysis has been the most difficult problem. With from two to half a dozen personalities, the first problem was to find the original. Even in dual personality it has sometimes been found that what had been supposed to be the normal was not so.

In demonism there are usually two clear-cut personalities and analysis is simple. The Satanic personality often conceives itself as multiple when not so. Thus No. claimed to be a hundred and twenty-five demons, later reduced to five. The 'legion' case of the New Testament seems to be similar. But there are cases of multiple demonism. The Magdalene is one. Among our New Zealand cases, Nos. 148 and 149 are clearly defined, and so also is No. 167 from Kausuh Province, China, reported by Miss S. J. Garland. In the treatment of the cases studied by scientists two objects are aimed at. First: The personalities must be reintegrated. The unity, the co-ordination prevailing in the normal personality must be restored. Second: There is the 'squeezing,' the getting rid of personalities such as were not parts of the original integer. The Sallies, the Margarets, the demons are not parts of the original whole, but what Prince calls hypnotic artifacts. Some of their powers and characteristics are parts of the original, but others are super-added by suggestion, by educative processes and experiences after the personalities were formed.

Both of these processes depend upon the general underlying all reintegrating of personalities, the subduing of the subconscious mind by the conscious. Functions permanent to the integrated personality again take their place. Functions extraneous or temporary are obliterated. Whether such obliterated qualities may be retained in the subconscious is a question on which we need not speculate.

This re-establishing of the authority of the conscious

mind, in some of the cases studied by scientists, has resulted automatically, i.e., from unknown causes, shocks, etc. In treating the cases science has followed chiefly two lines. First: Neuro-psychic stimulus. The primary is invoked, interchange of personalities is encouraged.

In the case of Mr. Hanna, Sidis brought him out of the dull routine of the country town to a stimulating experience in New York, not shocking him with new experiences, but putting him among places and people with whom his former life bad been associated and intensifying the stimulus by a gay crowd in a restaurant, with music and jokes. He also used drugs- cannabis India, coffee, with mechanical stimulus- cold water, motion, etc. But science finds, what our experience confirms, that suggestion is the chief reliance in handling dissociation.

In most of the cases healed by science hypnotism has been used. The Paris and Nancy Schools both used it. J. and P. Janet healed Marcelline and Blanche W. with it. At Morzinnes M. Constans found it effective. With Miss B., Prince found that what had appeared to be a distinct personality, B II, was the original hypnotized, and that this B II was a combination of the 'Saint" and "The Realist." What could be simpler than to unite them under hypnosis, and then reawaken the united personality? But here a difficulty arose. 'Sally' had herself learned hypnotic methods, and, resenting the prospect of extinction, interfered with Prince's efforts. When he got rid of Sally, then he reintegrated Miss B. by hypnotism. Sidis prefers to use what he calls hypnodization- a method not hypnotism, but also based on suggestion.

The patient does not come into the hypnotic state, the normal consciousness does not give way to the subconscious. The patient is told to lie down and relax. Quiet, monotony, subdued singing and reading induce a dreamy state, in which, the subconscious may be communicated with by discreet hints or questions. By this method exploratory work, analysis, psychic treatment is done.

As to the treatment of demonism, for the first twenty years of my life in China, I was, like others, skeptical on the whole subject, and so cases were not often brought to me. Family skeletons usually prefer closets- But an old colporteur, Tai Shi Rung, having simple faith in the Bible, when he came in touch with the demonized, began to pray over and heal them. We could not but follow suit. Of the more than three hundred cases we have met the larger part have been healed. Other missionaries report similar experiences. A striking case of healing was that of No. 7. For three years his trade as carpenter had been laid aside. A demon afflicted him, telling him, as he afterwards reported to me, "You are suffering. Do you not know how to die?" To prevent suicide, his wife took away his belt and ankle-bands, cut off his queue, and watched him.

In 1906 two of his neighbors became Christians. They prayed with him, and he was healed. The healing occupied in all thirteen days. I saw him a few weeks later, smiling, well, and have often seen him in these years since the healing.

My No. 6, the wife of a carpenter, was desperately ill. The trouble began in the fourth month, 1915. She had been a widow of rather better social standing than he. Hence arose worry about the marriage. There seems also to have been female trouble. Spells of demonism would come on, usually at night, and last till daybreak. She would have pain. The speech would become thick and confused, the sight blurred. She could not eat. In the seventh month diarrhea set in. By the eighth month- late August, early September- she was bedridden, emaciated, sallow. The husband went fifteen miles for Elder Chen Ya Koh. He replied that he was coming to their village in three or four days

for the Sunday, and would see her then. The husband insisted
that she would not hold out so long. Mr. Chen said: "Well, I will
come right on." The next day, the husband met him, saying: "It is
all right now. The demon said, 'I am going,' and she has gotten
well." When I saw her on December 31st of that year, she was
ruddy, smiling, happy, well, and has been so for several years
since.

In April 1920, a man, No. 408, was brought on a boat to
the chapel at the K'wai village. He had been abed twenty-six
days, and for twenty odd had not been able to eat. His head hurt,
waist hurt, legs hurt, the pains changing from one place to
another and having no assignable cause. He was evidently on the
point of death. When the boat reached the chapel, the Christians
helped him inside. The church service was held. At the close the
Christians told him he could walk, and he immediately did so.
Ke walked to the boat, ate food, and on the way home even
prepared his own food. No. 124 continued well and intimate with
the missionaries until her death ten or twelve years after the
occurrence. Miss Margaret King reports No. in. She was
afflicted, and under the influence made away with several of her
own children. She, too, since becoming a Christian more than
fifteen years ago, has continued well and raised her family. The
cases of multiple demonism are also sealed, and in the same way.
Canon Williams' case, No. 148, was a bright girl in the mission
school. Her teachers often noted in her another personality, but
thought she was acting it. On coming up for confirmation a third
personality came forward, which would answer "No" to all
questions. She was not confirmed. Later on, during a mission she
asked for prayer that she might "be able to believe in Jesus
again." On being questioned, the same control manifested itself.
Finally she was asked a question to which the characteristic "no"
could not be answered. She was seized with a violent convulsion,
becoming absolutely rigid. A few minutes were occupied by the
friends in prayer and exorcising the demon in the name of Jesus.

DEMONISM

She was set completely free. She has since testified that she was conscious of the spirits, and that one of them would not let her believe in Jesus.

The cases of demonism, simple or multiple, which have not been healed, were generally those which did not get a grasp of Christian principles and faith in Jesus Christ. Some cases may have been lost from physical complications which had become permanent. In treating demonism, medication should be used for what it is worth. Attendant or excitatory maladies being relieved, the patient is better able to master the psychic trouble. Furthermore, confidence in the practitioner may have a psychic effect. My first-aid box is so well known that I am called on for 'demon pills' on all occasions.

Except for the dangers of amateurism, I would use psychotherapeutic methods where indicated. Indeed, with No. 435 I did risk hypnotization, taking care to give the contra-suggestion before putting her to sleep. When she was in one of her tantrums, I suddenly remembered how Barker in the Johns Hopkins Hospital one day handled a hysteric. My nurse- for I was myself a patient at that time- told me of it with glee. So with this in mind, I told No. 435 that she would go to sleep and presently wake up with the demon gone. Then in the name of Jesus I ordered her to go to sleep. She was standing close to the pulpit. Directly she began to look drowsy. I had the seats removed and gently let her down on the platform. Taking up my sermon where the demon had interrupted me, I was trying to gather up the threads of the discourse, when she rolled over, calling in the most natural way, 'Mother, Mother,' and rose up normal.

But with demonism psychotherapeutic methods alone are not adequate. With No. 476, I again tried Barker's method. The case had every indication of being simple demonic hysteria.

DEMONISM

The woman, fifty or sixty years of age, had been afflicted only a month or so. She was abed, the chief symptoms being the variable hysteric pains and fright. There was no fever, nor were there rheumatic or other pathological symptoms. The witch had told her she would certainly die with it. The face was wild with terror, and the pulse racing. During the interview, she several times rose up with an expression on her face which looked almost as if the demon had taken control, but as she spoke only in the normal personality I did not address myself to the demon. I was confident that we could heal it, working on the normal personality by contra-suggestion. We took away the idols, told the family to believe in Jesus, prayed with them, and attempted to put her to sleep. That my methods were correct, so far as they went, was evident because at once the pulse slowed down, she yawned and became drowsy. But she did not succumb, and presently, at her request we withdrew, thinking she would fall asleep when the room got quiet. As we left, a worker, experienced with demonism, remarked, "You did not frighten him. He will not go unless you scare him." She did not sleep, any to speak of, nor has she recovered. On thinking back, I see that with No. 435 the hypnotization was successful after we had been working several days directly on the demon. In this case I failed to bring the name 'Jesus' to bear on the demon, and this explains the failure. We have seen that the demons fear Jesus. With Dr. Wood's case the mere mention of the name relieved the trouble at once. Ordinarily, I do not hesitate to order the demons in the name of Jesus to come out. In all our dealings with the trouble, we seek by prayer to become ourselves filled with faith in Jesus and to communicate this faith to the demonized.

In doing so we are working on scientific principles. We endeavor I. To educate in Christian principles; II. To develop Christian habits; III: To produce and intensify the conviction that Jesus can heal. Thus, scientifically considered, the consciousness, the primary personality, is by suggestion and stimulus enabled to overcome the subconscious, Satanic personality... for it is thus that the power of the Son of God works. All association with and reliance upon idolatry must be broken off. A distinct advance is made when the nose-ring is taken off, and the vegetarian vows broken. They are links with the old superstitious life. A Christian parent, brother, or husband, means much to the case. A little prayer, even though not understood, is a habit former, not to speak of the deeper significance of it. It was pathetic to hear the conglomeration of prayer and hymn that ignorant No. 2 used. "Jesus save my heart and life. Jesus save my life. Jesus loves me, I love Jesus. Jesus, pity me a sinner. Thank- thank- a sinner."

Coming to church is most important. It draws out the willpower and strengthens faith. In the case of No. 2, as soon as a spell came on, the Christians would hurry her into the chapel. When visiting a patient at the home, our workers would sometimes take a group of schoolboys along to sing. With No. 1, a motto was pasted over the bed: "Jesus saves me." With No. 33, to overcome the aboulia about eating, Mr. Tai assured the family that if he handed bread to the patient, the demon could not interfere. She took it, ate, and soon recovered. An essential of success is confidence on the part of the operator. This is in line with the principle brought out by Sidis that with normal persons, the critical faculties have to be evaded by indirect suggestion, but that with a subject under hypnotism, being already in a condition of abnormal suggestibility, direct suggestion should be used. The voice of the operator should be authoritative, commanding. A timid, doubtful manner is not effective. Hence the success of the simple-minded Christians. They are not troubled by doubts and queries, as the missionary is, unless he has studied the matter out to a clear conviction. In the long run his conviction, based on intelligence, is more stable than their unenlightened faith.

DEMONISM

A word as to non-Christian exorcisms. They owe what apparent success they may seem to have to the misuse of this principle of suggestion. To tell a patient with convincing assurance that the demon will relieve the pain on condition of the burning of so much incense does give temporary relief, but at the price of intensifying the thralldom. The supposed case of tetanus (No. 108) was so relieved. So also with No. 109 the paralysis passed off, but afterwards the patient testified to being utterly wretched in bondage. When finally healed by Christianity, she became normal- and free.

Efforts to frighten, force, or tempt the demon to leave are, of course, futile. With No. 73 they fired a gun to frighten the fox away. With No. 58 they placed the poor woman in a cesspool up to the neck for a long time. With Nos. 79, 80, and 81 , the exorcist tried to entice the demon to his own home. In Moslem lands they have a curious medley of superstitious practices known as a 'zar,' which is supposed to relieve the demonized. The puerilities and cruelties of so-called Christians in former times need not be reviewed. V. In treating cases of demonism one is liable to be discouraged by difficulties. Jesus' disciples, too found some cases more difficult to heal than others. Complications, psychic or physical, may occur. My No. 8 seemed to have tuberculosis. With No. 17 one leg and one arm had been paralyzed for years. Nos. 85, 88 and others had asthmatic complications. Knowing, as we now do, that asthma is itself a psychic condition, we are not surprised that demonism should light it up. Complications often clear up with no specific treatment when the demonism is healed.

Female cases seem more difficult than male. We have seen (Chap. IV) that the predisposition of females to demonism is due rather to the psychic than to the physical feminine. But both psychic and physical conditions may complicate matters. The readiness with which males recover may be seen, e.g., in my

DEMONISM

No. 86. This man was troubled for years. He could neither walk nor eat. Friends brought him to church in a boat. Yet the next Sunday he walked in several miles. When I saw him a few weeks later, he was normal. Indeed I could not pick him out in a crowd. So also Nos. 407, 408, men, cleared up quickly and easily. But the case of No. 72, a bright, strong, young woman, was protracted for several years. Nos. 4 and 5, both females, each took a year to recover. Cases of long duration seem to be relatively difficult. Thus No. 58, whose case has come down through three generations from mother-in-law to daughter-in-law, was under our treatment a year or more, while her neighbor, No. 68, also a woman, a case of only a few months, cleared up readily, and she was soon rejoicing in a baby- her first one. This is simply due to the fact that a belief, a conviction of three generations standing is harder to eradicate than one of three months.

What I have called reflective cases are usually not so difficult. When No. 79, already afflicted, was married, her husband also became afflicted, and later a child. The demon would speak out, now in one and now it; another of the family, the demonism of the original case being reflected, as it were, in the other members of the family. The husband was easily healed, but the wife's case took several years. Circumstances of various kinds may hinder recovery. With Nos. 5, 77 and others, poverty prevented attendance on church in busy seasons and backsets occurred. A number of cases, 83, 122 and others, after making satisfactory progress, meeting family friction were angered, and anger is liable to light it up. When the primary personality of the patient, whether through fear and helplessness or through moral perversity, assumes a supine attitude, there is not much hope until that is overcome. A case of this kind is No. 105, reported by Miss Waterman. The patient, when normal, showed no desire to be healed and made no effort.

DEMONISM

The great difficulty with treating demonism today is the prevalence and the tenacity of polytheism, and the hostility on racial grounds to Christianity. In Judea monotheism was universal, and in spite of political opposition faith in Jesus was strong and growing. Some of our cases have been lost because ignorant friends took them back under idolatrous environment, Perseverance and faith usually overcome even in difficult cases. No. 65 is a woman, and one who had been afflicted twenty-nine years. None of the family were Christians. When the affliction came on, it would feel like something pushing along up the face, shoving the mouth and nose upwards. There would be a sensation as of hammering on the top of the head. Sometimes the distress would be so great that she would roll on the floor. In 1917 she was led to come to church. The Christians tried to teach her a prayer, but she could not remember it. The demon talked vociferously at the church. On December 9th, 1917, I was at Tienhu. I noticed in a room opposite several women. The Elder Ch'en came out of there, remarking: "Even here she is still talking strange talk," i.e., the demon talk. When she came before the session, I saw her to be a woman well-built and healthy-looking except that one eye was drawn up in a nervous tension and the head was nodding. The report indicated clearly a case of demonism, which she had failed thus far to overcome. I gave her a sentence prayer which she could remember.

On May 18th, 1918, she walked six miles to church, coming in hot but not exhausted, to all appearances normal and reporting no trouble since the last interview. The next day she was baptized. Just afterwards, during a long congregational meeting, I noticed a commotion. She was having a spell. The face was drawn up, the eyes looked distraught, she twisted in distress. There was now no talking by the Satanic personality. A 'dumb' demon does not signify necessarily that the patient is chronically dumb, though that may sometimes result from demonism, but that under the influence the patient cannot talk.

DEMONISM

So evident were the symptoms- after we had been working on her nearly a year- that missionaries present, who had before been non-committal, after the service frankly admitted conviction of the reality of demonism. To prevent confusion at the time I called for Mr. Tai. He sat by her, holding her hand, and the spell passed off.

On June 23rd, 1918, I was again at Tienhu, and held long services, but there was no further trouble nor has there been since that time.

My observation is that cases which have gotten a real faith in Jesus have, as a rule, been healed. In comparing these modern cases with those healed by Jesus, question may be raised as to the time element. His cases seem to have been healed immediately; ours sometimes take months or years. Does this indicate difference in the affection or in the treatment? The facts show that the affection is the same, and as to the treatment the difference is relative not absolute. We do not know what is included in the record of New Testament cases. Workers report to me that on such and such a date a patient was healed. I find on investigation what they mean is that the patient then grasped the faith, made the turning-point, passed the crisis, though it may have taken time for the convalescence to be completed. It would be no discredit to the records to suppose that some of Jesus' cases had backsets.

Our cases are sometimes healed immediately. No. 101, as reported by Dr. Woods, was healed in rive minutes. No. 108, as reported by Miss King, after several ineffectual attempts, finally made a definite decision, burnt her idols, and from that time was healed. Nos. 35, 37, 62, 68, 73, 113, 129, 145, 149, 150, 302, 407, 408 and others are reported as immediate cures. The process with us, as with Jesus, is clearly a matter of suggestion, but not having His divine power, with us an educative process is sometimes necessary before the suggestion can take effect. Indeed, Emanuel Geijerstam reports from the scientific standpoint that in many cases of hysteria and neurasthenia treated by him the hypnotic methods used only started the ameliorative process and complete restoration followed in the course of time.

The superior efficacy of Jesus' treatment is easily understood.

I. The psychic attitude of the community affects the situation. We note that in China where the church is strong and growing, where the sentiment of the community tends strongly towards the church, the demonized are more readily healed than elsewhere.

II. A given method in the hands of a master is pre-eminently effective. A demon which could resist the disciples dare not resist Jesus the Christ.

CHAPTER XI

Treatment of Demonomanias

As to the treatment of the insanities which resemble demonism, I make bold to put forward a broad proposition. Others may have anticipated me, but if so, it has not come to my knowledge.

In Chap. VI we reviewed some of the prominent theories as to diseases of psychic origin. My proposition is that under all of these systems a most powerful curative factor is the leading of the mind into a healthy, normal religious life. Suppose we think with Dubois and would correct mental abnormalities by an educative process, leading men into right and normal attitudes of mind and of conduct. Indisputably one of the deepest human impulses, the most inexorable cravings is for something to satisfy the religious nature. Can we, then, expect the mentality to function properly, if we leave out this element or antagonize it?

Or let us adopt the libido terminology. Christians who incline to psychoanalytic views need have no hesitation in recognizing this principle of the libido, the flow of biological energy manifested in desire. If God made man, implanting in him the fixed necessity of perpetuating the species and providing for the transmission by heredity of physical and psychic qualities, then the libido also can just as readily be attributed to Divine origin. Deep in the heart of this libido, as all scientists admit, is the craving for God. Jung himself recognizes it as a biological necessity. Speaking of the religious-philosophical attitude he says: "This attitude is itself an achievement of civilization; it is a function that is exceedingly valuable from a biological point of view, for it gives rise to the incentives that force human beings to do creative work for the benefit of a future age, and, if necessary, to sacrifice themselves for the welfare of the species." He and some other psychoanalysts do not recognize religion as based on fact, but as a process of emotional sublimation. But whatever view we take, we find ourselves confronted with the fact that religion is one of the most powerful factors of the libido.

On the principles of these several schools, it is interference with the libido, obstruction of the libido, overstrain in adjustments for the libido, that cause trouble. Is it not the logical corollary that provision for the full, untrammeled flow of the libido along one of its favorite channels must make for normal conditions? This religious life is not to be developed by mere enforcement of authority, by ecclesiasticism. The spirit of Jesus Christ must be implanted in the life, the spirit of love, and also of desire to do God's will. The craving for a God on whom to rely must find a solid resting place.

Or take Prince's view of emotive impulse causing psychic conflict, and Sidis's view of nerve exhaustion from fear. Religion wrongly taught may lead to worry, to abnormal fear, to overanxiety, and thus to psychopathic conditions. But on the other hand, religion rightly understood is a guide to the emotions and a palliative for overwrought nerves. It has been said that sex and religion are the two greatest emotive impulses, both bearing on the perpetuation of life, or conversely expressed, both arising from fear of extinction, The satisfying of these two cravings in normal, right ways goes far to satisfy, and thus to regulate the powerful emotions, and also to conserve the nerve force by relieving worry and fear. Man cannot get rid of the great unknown. Trouble, affliction, sorrow, death press in on us at every turn. Religion allays, relieves, comforts, strengthens.

On one occasion President McKinley had been on a heavy mental strain. He had by force of will kept at it until midnight. As he lay down the work, McKinley broke out in an exclamation, "I could not stand this sort of thing if it were not for God to rely on." This expresses the experience of the greatest men. Hence I claim that religion wisely presented is a psychopathic sedative and tonic. There are functional insanities in which it may relieve the conditions entirely.

When permanent organic changes have taken place, religion may help, even where it cannot heal. Mrs. A. H. Smith reports No. 130. A meat peddler and his wife had lived amicably, so far as known. One day he came home arbitrary and unreasonable from drink. She talked back. He struck her. They fought and she went off into violent insanity, breaking windows, etc. It took three men to hold her. Her supply of milk dried up, and the baby had to go to others. Later the violence lessened but she continued insane. The husband could hardly keep any clothes on her. She could not sleep, reviled people. Finally she was sent to the mission hospital. Christian friends made it a subject for earnest prayer.

The husband resisted their influence. But finally he made a confession of his sin in striking the woman and prayed. Both now had full religious life, and in a few days the woman went home sane. Another case given by Mrs. Smith, No. 142, seems to be incipient insanity, relieved by the mind going into a current of smooth religious life. This was a young man of Christian parentage. He had been well educated and looked forward to going to America. But he drifted away from religion. He began to do strange things. His head troubled him. The jangle of voices in the neighbor's yard worried him till he threw brickbats over the wall. He struck an invalid boy and an old woman. He would strike and revile children, would fly into a passion if a meal was late, break dishes, etc. A shelter was built for him outside the city wall and he took to herding goats. But he could still hear the church bell, and once ordered the keeper not to ring it, thus showing that conscience about religious matters was back of his trouble. One day in silent meditation, he seemed to have a change of heart. He wanted work. So he was set to writing and teaching. As he studied the Bible he became repentant, prayed, began to go to church. Confession to those he had struck and worried relieved him.

At one time he omitted going to church and trouble began again; he broke lamp chimneys, dishes, a mirror stand. Again under prayer of friends he revived. The writing out of his experiences for this book gave him an upward lift, and he is now recovered. Miss Mary Culler White gives a case of insanity with physical conditions which was helped by religion and Christian treatment. She had noticed a wretched-looking woman, who was nagged about by hoodlums. When Miss White was one day telling non-Christian ladies about prayer, they challenged her with the question, "Why do you not pray for that woman?" She did. At that time she feared to take the woman in, lest she be criticized. In January 1919, she again felt moved to try Christianity on this case. Sending out, she found the woman's lair, for she lived like a beast. The next day the woman wandered near the mission while revival services were going on. Miss White took her in. The patient was 27 years old. She had been sold about from one man to another. Insanity came on after the birth and death of a child. An eye had been lost, as was said, through smallpox. She was in a horrible state, filthy, hair cut off, her naked body showing no appearance of her sex. She had a bad case of syphilis. She showed no alternations of personality but outbursts of temper. In her tantrums she would chant like the demonized. For a time she forgot her own name and the place where she had lived. There was bitter antagonism to the name Jesus. The Chinese classified her as mentally afflicted rather than demonized.

The missionaries placed chief reliance on Christianity.

DEMONISM

The day she was taken in, they gave her a bath, a place to sleep, and held special prayers over her. The next morning they noticed improvement already. After a time the woman ceased her antagonism and herself prayed to Jesus. In April the missionaries set a day, invited friends from other cities and spent the day in prayer for her. By 4 p.m. she was distinctly quieter and from that date a marked change was noticeable. For her physical condition they used drugs, with injections of soamin. By August the syphilitic symptoms had ceased and the drugs were stopped. But the mind was still not right and the treatment by Christian influence was continued. After nineteen months in the mission she was quiet, sweet-tempered, spent her time spinning and making grass ropes- well, but a little simple-minded. (Ulus. 15.)

My No. 202 is a case of demonomania in America. How the patient was diagnosed and treated in the hospital I am not informed. He relates his experience as follows. He was brought up in a Christian home, but took to drink and became an infidel in religion. During a wild life he began to believe himself possessed of demons.

He thought he saw Satan, thought people or demons were trying to poison him, were trying to squirt the poison on him or to bore holes in the floor and thus reach him. He was put in an asylum. After a time he perceived that the demons were deceiving him with falsehoods. He got a Bible and read it. He would silently argue with the demons. He would pray publicly all about the place, until he read about praying in your closet, and saw that in this also he had been misled of the Devil. For a time the thought was borne in on him that he was the Apostle Peter. In childhood the name bad been impressed on his memory by a boy making a joke of it. This he argued out, saying that Peter was holy but he was wicked, and thus it could not be. He also worked out the question about Millennial Dawnism. Finding a book of Cowper's he was helped by that. In time he was healed and now for some years has preached the Gospel. The struggles of this bewildered mind to right itself evidently found help by religious lines of thought. Granting that the hospital treatment, whatever it was, may have been suited to his needs, we can see how religion was an effective psychic influence. I put forth my proposition, in the hope that others more competent may take it up, and work it out scientifically.

CHAPTER XII

Prevention

The principles we have now worked out open up before us a vast field for social psychotherapeutics. A few of us have been in these demon haunts. We have seen cases like the 'Skeleton Child,' all wasted away with what appeared to be disease, brought back to life and health by getting rid of the demon. We know that the multitudes are in psychic slavery to the wizards and witches, and that they themselves are in bondage. My No. 120 was widely known as 'The Wizard.' Years ago he had suddenly gone to bed, desperately ill and talking idiot-like. For ten years he was compelled to practice wizardry, himself, his wife and son all suffering with periodic attacks of demonism. But Jesus healed them and made him a herald of freedom. There are millions afflicted by, and billions in dread of this curse. And all could be averted. The world could be freed from this bondage. The great heart of mankind will respond to this need when it is appreciated.

To a fire, to a famine, to a war, we rush with relief, regardless of cost; we organize museums and societies for scientific research ; we endow universities and hospitals for the relief of human ignorance and human ills. We who have been delivered from the thralldom of medievalism need only to see this curse under which two-thirds of the human race are in bondage. We cannot go by on the other side and leave them to some Samaritan's care.

In order to this relief, the first consideration is that the thinking world should understand the subject. Others, it is to be hoped, will follow up the lead I have here given. Light is needed on many points and it will take further testimony to convince an incredulous world of the facts. A subject of such proportions would justify the lifelong study of competent men. Exploratory expeditions would be worth while, but unless wisely directed their data would be worthless. True demonism is elusive. In a very shoal of demons, investigators would catch none unless they knew how. Special departments for the study of this branch of psychiatry are a distinct desideratum. Especially should there be provision for the receiving and publishing of facts on this subject.

To get rid of demonism the one essential is to free mankind from the belief that spiritualities can and do 'possess' men ad libitum. How shall we go about this? The answer comes trippingly on somebody's tongue, Teach that there are no spiritualities. But note, to do this we must face:

I. The belief of the Christian world on grounds of faith that there are spiritualities.

The proofs now being put forward on scientific grounds to the persistence of the personality after death.

III. The proofs we ourselves have seen herein.

IV. The incontrovertible fact that no civilization has yet been established on the no-spirituality basis, a fact which shows that belief in spiritualities is part of our being.

The psychanalysts admit this fact and attempt to account for it as a biological product, as sublimation of the libido. But that there are no spiritualities, that nature, the libido, God, would infix in us an indestructible belief in a lie, even for worthy, utilitarian purposes, is a hypothesis which is incapable of demonstration and unacceptable to the mind of humanity. We cannot believe that there would be appetite were there no food for thirst were there no drink, sexual desire were there no sex, avarice were there no money, fellow feeling were there no fellows, ponging for a fictitious God is a theory unworthy of the science of biology. What can be done, what must be done is to get rid of the false superstitious ideas as to what spiritualities there are. The fox demons and weasel demons and pig demons must follow the ghosts and wraiths and banshees into oblivion. Tales of the weird must be brought to the bar of exact truth. The ancient worship of bulls and cats, of he-goats, of the seminal principle, of Jupiter and Mercury, and all the rest of them has long since given way to recognition of God, a worship satisfying to the strongest minds of the race. Furthermore, the powers and limitations of spiritualities must be defined, We must bring the spirit world under the reign of law. Men must be taught that, granting the continued existence after death of a father in law or an enemy, he has no power to 'possess' a poor girl of his own volition.

If spirits, without regard to law or to God, the author of law, had the power to communicate with men at will, our departed friends would habitually meet us around the fireside. That they do not is itself proof that there is restriction, that law regulates their course. That God may let down the bars for a Samuel is easily conceivable. That there are laws unknown to us which would in some cases temporarily loose the restrictions, it is not possible to deny without proof. If so, we could understand some of those phenomena observed by the Societies for Psychic Research. But we can absolutely deny that spirits are free from law.

The hypothesis that Satan has the power to send departed spirits to earth seems hardly credible. We saw in Chapter IX that probably he can utilize evil spiritualities, non-human, both to tempt men to sin and also to cause dissociation in those weakened by fear. But spirits of the wicked dead are, of course, subject to restrictions, as others are. Recognition of the reign of law in the spiritual world will do away with demonism. It will disabuse the idea that ghosts walk the earth ad libitum, and also that Satan can 'possess' whom he will. Remove the fear of being demonized, and we remove demonism. Men can be hypnotized, but we do not live in fear of it. The belief that demons can 'possess,' regardless of the attitude of mind of the subject, leads to fear, and the fear induces the attitude of 'expectant attention,' the very thing which renders men liable to demonization. Knowledge will relieve fear. Above all, the worship of the dead, of saints and demons, of imaginary spirits, all forms of polytheism, must be given up. Sentimental attempts to whitewash medievalism are criminal. The 'Light of Asia' is the blackness of Inferno. As well eulogize indiscriminate venesection, such as hastened the death of Washington, or put the science of medicine back in the hands of the barbers. The chirurgeons were, doubtless, well meaning men, but many a death must be laid to their door.

Here let me give a most serious and friendly warning. The Societies for Psychic Research maintain the continued existence of personalities after death and the possibility of their taking control of living men. As a matter of scientific study, the importance of their investigations can hardly be overestimated. But we should note that they are working with poisons- as science has to do. The use of these poisons is entirely another matter. Some attempt to utilize these spirits. Hence arises Spiritualism- which many confuse with the scientific work of the Societies. Appeal to spirits, whether their existence be proven or not, is of the nature of worship. It is just what the Chinese do when they pray to a man named Kwau, canonized as the God of War, or to a man named Chang, canonized as the Jade Emperor. It is the seeking after those 'that peep and that mutter.' This is the curse which God taught the Jews of old to fight. If such practices spread, demonism will result.

DEMONISM

Rev. Canon Williams states that two English ladies, coming under the influence of New Zealand Spiritualism, became demonized. As this chapter goes to press, I see in "The Healer,' London, July 1921, a case of demonism in New England, reported by a Catholic priest. It bears all the marks of genuineness. The patient is a woman of fifty years. At the first word of exorcism- doubtless the name 'Jesus' was used- she was seized with convulsive shivering. In the exorcism there were numerous ejections. There was speech in different languages, which the priest took to be medieval Italian and Hindustani. With each ejection the face would be twisted into a 'devilish' appearance; there would be heavings and chokings. There were periods of rigidity. This woman formerly had had no trouble and did not believe in spirits other than God. But one summer she rented her cottage on the seacoast to spiritualists for a 'camp meeting.' When she came back into the house, trouble began.

Now, whether it was due to spirits invoked or to auto-suggestion, after she had heard of what had been done, in any case it must be attributed to the practices of the spiritualists. Let science and religion beware. Demonism will come in Christian lands, if the practice of appealing to spirits becomes common.

In this matter of demonism governments bear heavy responsibility. To what extent are they to exert civil power for the removal of degrading moral and religious conditions? Here we touch the delicate line between religious freedom and civic betterment. Modern civilization is based on the policy of religious freedom and non-interference by the government in church matters. Yet no one would question that it was the duty of the British Government to abolish the suttee and the Juggernaut in India. Considerations of personal liberty cannot excuse robbery and murder. Malpractice is murder. It is so construed under enlightened governments. Cases have come before the Western courts of death resulting because a father or mother, with erroneous views about faith healing, has refused to call in the physician. Can the courts remit responsibility in such cares because of religious errors?

How can governments deal with demonism? Sympathetic support can be given to healthy religious and moral education. As to superstitious practices, at least official sanction should be withheld. Government officials who encourage and participate in idolatrous processions and worship of idols on feast days, who consult necromancers as to dates, who raise funds for the building of temples, are thereby bringing misery on many of their people. And indeed, it is the duty of a government to suppress idolatry and witchcraft. We should outlaw malpractice in religion just as in medicine. The old Jewish law of capital punishment for witchcraft, when misinterpreted and misapplied, has wrought injustice and misery. Yet the intent of it was, not to give credence to witchcraft, but to stop those who were corrupting the nation with superstitious practices. Had not the Jews put away witchcraft and idolatry, the probability is that we should still be on a par with China as to superstition, demonism, and degraded religious practices. We owe more to that old drastic legislation than we appreciate.

In this day we do not stone criminals nor crucify them, yet law must be enforced. An enemy who should spread the germs of tetanus or tuberculosis would find short shrift when caught. America now prohibits alcohol because it degrades mentally and physically. By the same tokens witchcraft, fortune-telling, idolatry, which cause this form of insanity, should be forbidden.

In this social therapeutics education is an important factor. Unwise or ignorant theologians, who do not comprehend this fact, may obstruct progress. It was a church which killed the Christ because He was enlightening them. It was a church which

DEMONISM

forced Galileo to recant the Copernican views and with texts of Scripture fought down Columbus in the Spanish Junta. Science is not an enemy of true religion but an ally. Psychiatrists, students of abnormal psychology, have opened up a wider field than they knew. Psychic abnormalities in Western lands are those of the individual, the result, it may be, of peculiar nervous and mental conditions, of family environment, of heredity, of organic or functional defects, and what not. Demonism is psychopathology en masse. Here psychotherapeutics must be on a large scale. In this work students, journalists, authors must take the lead. And the progress of civilization is an unconscious social remedy. Ships and railroads, commercial and diplomatic intercourse, athletics and travel are all demonicides.

But in the long run, true religion must be the final remedy. As I have said, human history shows no case of a civilization without a religion. Experiments along this line, as, e.g., in the French Revolution, proved chimerical. Renan admitted that there could be no civilization without a religion. From a scientific as well as a historical point of view, we may see that religion is necessary to relieve demonism. Nature abhors a psychic vacuum. Demonism originates in suggestion, and suggestion must be used to cure it. This is the Divine remedy. This is Jesus Christ's panacea for demonism, which has proved so effective. Faith in him will cleanse China and Japan and India and Africa and New Zealand and the Moslem lands of demonism.

The thinkers of China do not believe in demons. Any cultured Chinese will quote you the well-known couplet: "If you believe in the gods, they are; if you believe not, they are not." The literati resisted the introduction of Indian Buddhism and still theoretically oppose it. Yet the land is full of idols, and they themselves worship them. Negations cannot nullify misreligion. Confucianism had nothing positive to offer. There is need of something to give contra-suggestion and thus drive out the fear of demons.

There is in the human make-up a psychic necessity for religion- for a. religion strong enough to make men die for it, yet free and intelligent.

The impulses of the human mind, given direction towards higher ideals, towards wisdom, towards love, reach out and lay hold on God. Failing this, men's minds grow up in morasses of ignorance, superstition, evil. The enlightened form of Christianity provides the sociological corrective of demonism.

THE END

Made in the USA
Columbia, SC
11 June 2019